KRISTIN GRIFFITH

RUSH

memoir of a gay
SORORITY girl

ISBN ebook: 978-1-7355707-1-6

ISBN paperback: 978-1-7355707-0-9

First Edition

United States of America

Cover design and interior: Vanessa Mendozzi

Editor: Teja Watson

www.kristingriffith.com

To everyone who has ever felt like an outsider
It takes courage to be yourself
Celebrate your uniqueness and strength

AUTHOR'S NOTE

This book is based on extensive journals I kept, an article I wrote in the college student newspaper, a short story in an anthology I wrote a few years after I graduated from college, interviews with key characters, research, and sorority memorabilia and photos. I have changed the names of the individuals in this book, to maintain anonymity. There are no composite characters or events in this book. I have done my best to preserve the truth of every scene and every conversation.

CONTENTS

PART THREE - JUNIOR YEAR

PART FOUR - SENIOR YEAR

PROLOGUE: WANNA DANCE?

Junior Year, 1994

I hoped the shots of rum, screwdriver, and Bud Lights I drank before we left would give me the courage I needed tonight. I wasn't "out" in my sorority and, though I had brought my girlfriend, Sarah, to an informal event as a "friend," I had never slow danced with her or showed any PDA. I had never heard of any "out" gay sorority member in any of the seven sororities at my midwestern university. In fact, the only gay person in the Greek system I had heard about was kicked out of his fraternity when he came out.

I blurted, "Do you wanna dance?"

Looking surprised, Sarah stopped. "Really?"

"Yes."

I took a deep breath and felt a strong punch in the gut. Sarah slowly moved toward me and I moved toward her. I looked around to see if any of my sorority sisters were watching us. About 25 straight couples seemed engaged with each other, slow dancing in the grand hall on campus at our sorority pajama party. Our flannel pants and slippers fit in with the sea of boxers and sexy pajamas for the themed party.

We stopped close, face-to-face. Sarah didn't move and neither did I. Then I slowly placed my right hand on her left hip and my left hand on her right hip. Our eyes locked. She slowly reached her arms around my neck and asked, "Is this okay?"

I stammered, "Yes." Even as my stomach clenched harder, her touch sent warm shivers of pleasure down my body. Her arms circled my neck and she pulled in closer until our bodies touched. She rested her head on my left shoulder, nuzzling into my neck. I could feel her long brown hair brush against my skin.

My eyes remained wide open as one by one, the stares started. I felt my face burn. Some people looked confused. Some looked angry. Some looked disgusted. I could see couples whisper to each other as they looked at us. Some couples pointed at us or stopped moving altogether. I couldn't see Sarah's face, since her head was nuzzled into my neck. *Did she feel the daggers aimed at us too?*

I didn't hear the music. Frowns hit me from all directions, so I avoided eye contact with everyone. I tried to focus on Sarah and enjoy the moment, but I couldn't—all I felt were the stares. I thought about sprinting out of the hall. It was like the dreams I had in elementary school where I found myself on stage naked while everyone laughed at me; in the dreams, I would run off the stage in embarrassment. Now it felt like I was choosing to remain naked onstage and accept the laughs instead of running away and putting on clothes.

The song felt like it lasted an hour. When it finally ended, I avoided eye contact with everyone except Sarah. I quickly said to Sarah, "You ready to go?"

"Uh, sure."

As we bolted out the door, the searing wind slapped me in the face and whipped my long blond hair into my eyes. I took out a Marlboro Red, lit it, inhaled deeply and felt the bitter smoke in my lungs. As we walked back in silence, I smoked two more cigarettes in quick succession. Sarah looked at me with compassionate eyes as I took another drag.

Walking quickly, thoughts hurtled through my head. *What are people going to say tomorrow? How will I face everyone in my sorority? Will everyone be talking behind my back? Will I get kicked out?*

PART ONE

FRESHMAN YEAR

1

SORORITY RUSH

January, Freshman Year

Sororities were only for popular girls. I knew I'd never be in one. I pretended it was because I wanted it that way, but secretly I longed for that feeling of belonging I imagined sorority girls felt.

My first-choice college was Rice University in Houston, in part because they had no sororities or fraternities. All freshmen at Rice were randomly assigned to dorms or houses, and that was your social group. These "houses" threw parties, much like frats and sororities. But you didn't have to apply. You didn't have to be cool or confident to get in one—and you didn't have to get rejected if you weren't.

When a rejection letter from Rice squashed my dreams, I went with my second choice instead: Washington University in St. Louis. One third of Wash U students belonged to sororities or fraternities. I had loved the picturesque campus when I visited with my mom. When it came time to leave, I was excited, but also apprehensive, since I had never been away from home by myself before.

The first week of college, I walked back to my dorm room after

freshman orientation and the door stood ajar. Three guys in blue
uniforms turned to look at me. Black bags with what looked like
medical paraphernalia were scattered about, and my roommate,
Madison, lay on her bed barely moving.

In the profiles Wash U had sent to me about my randomly
assigned roommate, I had learned that Madison was a cheerleader
from Connecticut. She had long permed hair, wore tight Guess
jeans and a lot of pink. She was the kind of girl that made me feel
insecure—probably very popular, invited to all the cool parties,
with a boyfriend on the football team. Her bedspread was a pastel
floral print from Laura Ashley.

I, on the other hand, hailed from Austin, Texas, and wore baggy
jeans, tie-dye shirts, and black loafers. My long hair was often in
a ponytail because I didn't know what else to do with it. I had a
huge New Order poster on my wall, and I liked to dance in clubs
filled with fog machines, dark electronic music, and people wearing all
black. My bedspread was a bright red velour blanket, with black sheets.

Two old mattresses, two dressers, two desks, and two tiny closets
packed our 9x12-foot room in the co-ed freshman dorm. A dingy
rug covered the floor. The chipped furniture held years of students'
initials carved into it. It smelled of stale beer and mustiness from
decades of messy freshman.

One of the uniformed guys hovered over Madison. "Do you
know where you are?"

Madison, her eyes barely open, mumbled, "My dorm room?"
And then she started to vomit, all over her bed and the paramedic's
pants. It smelled like hot, rotting garbage.

One of the other EMTs turned to me and said, "Are you her
roommate?"

Still standing in the doorway, I nodded.

"We're from the emergency medical team on campus. Your roommate has alcohol poisoning."

I continued to stand in the doorway. "What does that mean?" I had only tasted alcohol twice in my life. Once, I snuck a Corona from my parent's fridge and didn't like it. Another time I reluctantly took a few sips of beer a guy gave me at a high school party senior year.

"She drank too much alcohol. From what I can tell, she must have had eight to twelve drinks tonight." That seemed like an insane amount of alcohol for someone who barely weighed a hundred pounds.

He continued. "I need you to watch her until the morning and check on her every couple of hours. Try to keep her lying on her side. If she starts vomiting while lying on her back, she could choke on it. Get her some water and ibuprofen in the morning. She will have a huge hangover. Does that all make sense?"

He handed me a card with a phone number printed on it. I took it, confused by all the instructions.

The EMT asked again, "Can you do that? Can you check on her all night?"

Feeling unsteady, I managed an "Okay." The three EMTs picked up their bags and left, leaving me with a room smeared with vomit and a roommate I barely knew, who was moaning every few minutes.

I sat on my bed facing her, on high alert in case she got sick again. At some point, I went to the women's bathroom, brushed my teeth, got some water for her, then changed into a pair of boxer shorts and a T-shirt. I turned off the light, got in my single bed, and stared at the ceiling. I asked, "Madison, are you okay?" She groaned. I took that as a good sign.

As I lay in bed trying not to fall asleep, I thought about my sister, Marsha. She was in an inpatient drug treatment center for cocaine addiction. I missed her, even though she hadn't really been my sister for a long time. I stared at my roommate and cried in the dark. I missed my sister. I missed my parents. And I didn't have any friends yet.

I didn't sleep at all that night. I woke Madison up every couple of hours, and the rest of the time I lay in bed staring at the ceiling. I had expected college would be this idyllic place, but now I got the feeling it would be more difficult than I thought.

In the morning, my roommate didn't remember anything, and we never talked about it.

A few months later during my freshman year, Becky, who lived on the same dorm floor, said, "Sorority rush is starting in January. Are you going to sign up?"

"No, definitely not. Why—are you?"

"Yes! My mom was in a sorority and I've always wanted to join. You should do it!"

"Oh, I don't think so. I mean, I've never really pictured myself in a sorority. And I doubt I'd get in."

Growing up, I was neither popular nor a complete outsider. Playing sports saved me from total outcast status, but my shyness, lack of confidence, and studiousness got in the way of popularity.

I was particularly short by Texas standards at only five-foot-two. My classmates loved to call me "shrimp." Even though my mom told me it would stunt my growth, I started drinking coffee in elementary school—adding spoonfuls of powdered creamer and sugar like my parents. On airline flights, when the flight attendant asked me what I wanted to drink and I said "coffee," she inevitably looked at nine-year-old me and said, "You're too young to drink coffee."

In second grade, I got my first pair of glasses, and to (unsuccessfully) avoid being called "Four Eyes," I tried to get away with not wearing them. This meant sitting in the first row in class—obviously not where the cool kids sat. Then, in sixth grade, my mom bought me a training bra from Sears, which I didn't yet need. Kids called me "sunken treasure chest." Ha ha. Very funny. It didn't help that my only sister joined in on the name-calling; she was a fan of "dork" and "dingleberry." Going to four different schools in five years (between eighth and twelfth grade) hadn't exactly helped with making friends either.

So, when Becky tried to convince me after dinner one night to sign up for rush, I was hesitant. Model-perfect smiling girls with their arms around each other covered the sorority flyer. They looked like they were having a lot of fun—but they didn't look like me.

When we got to the sign-up, three All-American, confident-looking young women stood behind a table. Becky was already writing out a check to give them, to pay for rush. Her mom was a member of the Kappa Alpha Theta sorority, so Becky had an advantage as a "legacy"—which gave her preferential treatment. I stood there, frozen, as my stomach churned. *These girls are so intimidating. There's no way I can do this.*

In this strange, surreal state, I found myself reaching into my backpack and pulling out my checkbook. I was never friends with popular girls before, but deep inside I hoped things could be different for me in college. That kernel of hope propelled me forward, despite my fear of rejection.

I looked at the sign-up sheet, four pages filled with names in bubbly cursive.

I took the blue pen and started to print my name—no bubbly cursive for me. But I hesitated at the first "i" in my name. I looked at the hearts and circles dotting other "i"s on the page. My hand shook as I added dots above all four of the "i"s in my name, like I always do. I couldn't bring myself to draw hearts above them. This small act of not-conforming was to be the first of many throughout college. I longed to fit in, but couldn't completely pretend to be someone I wasn't.

A few weeks later, as Becky and I walked toward the Women's Building, which housed all the sorority suites, bitter January winds cut through my coat and I stuffed my hands further into my pockets. Long shadows from barren trees streaked the dead grass. Hundreds of other freshmen walked along the same paths from the freshman dorms, like rows of ants flocking to a few crumbs of food. I fidgeted with my schedule for the first round of rush parties, folded in my pocket.

We were welcomed in by shouts of "Welcome to rush! Go right inside and we'll help you find your first party!" As we walked into the large red-brick building, my ears and fingertips began to defrost, tingling with little pinpricks. Hundreds of women crowded the entrance area; I could feel their excitement. Dozens of sorority girls in long-sleeve Greek-lettered shirts skittered about, with glowing grins on their faces.

One of them approached us and asked if we needed help finding our first party. After directing Becky to Kappa Kappa Gamma, she looked at me. "What about you?"

I slowly unfolded my crumpled schedule and timidly read, "Delta

Gamma?"

She directed me there, then said, "Good luck! You'll do great!"

I doubted I would "do great!", but managed to get my feet moving. We headed toward the open, expansive stairway, filled with dozens of women moving up and down, the clicking of their heels barely audible over all the excited voices.

As Becky headed to Kappa Kappa Gamma, I walked until I saw DELTA GAMMA on a massive sign. Greek letters ΔΓ in pink and light blue adorned the door, next to perky girls wearing shirts that also said DELTA GAMMA.

"Welcome to Delta Gamma! We have the best group of girls here! You're gonna love it!"

I got in line behind a few dozen other people, stuck my hands in my pockets, and looked around, feeling on edge. A sea of fashionable girls in skirts and heels chatted with each other at epic decibels. I looked down at my jeans, Docksiders, and sporty sweater. The familiar feeling of not fitting in washed over me like a crashing wave. I owned exactly one skirt, one dress, and two pairs of heels—all of which I hated passionately—and no makeup. My mind shouted at me, "You don't belong here!"

As the rush leaders shouted, "Get ready everyone!" "Get excited!" I clenched my fists in my pockets. *Why did I think this was a good idea?*

I had always felt invisible and generic—the opposite of my younger sister, Marsha. She wore all the fashionable clothes. I didn't think to ask for clothes other than what my mom bought me at Sears. Marsha listened to cutting-edge bands like the Cure, Danzig, and Depeche Mode. I knew nothing about music. She was President of her seventh-grade class. I blended into the background. I envied her charisma and confidence and tried to copy her, even though she was younger.

But she wasn't here for me to follow now.

A few minutes later, the door opened and cheerful girls in matching pink ΔΓ shirts started singing a song and clapping loudly as they whisked us inside the packed suite. As I was enveloped by a frenzy of girls, one of the pink shirts introduced herself and handed me a plate holding a sugar cookie with ΔΓ on it in pink and blue, and a plastic cup of pink lemonade. The attack of friendliness felt warm but overwhelming.

The girl volleyed questions at me, rapid fire. "What classes are you taking?"

"Um, I'm taking Art History, Calculus II, a philosophy seminar, Astronomy to fulfill our science requirement, and our required writing class."

"What extracurricular activities do you like?"

"Uh, so, I play on an intramural soccer team right now. I like to play cards with my friends from my dorm too, but I guess that isn't really an extracurricular activity."

When I looked around the small suite, I saw huge framed pictures on the walls with photos of each member of the sorority, and the year at the bottom. They all wore the exact same black draping and looked almost identical.

At the end of the 45-minute party, we were ushered out and greeted in the hallway by rush advisers, who helped us find our next party. The suites all looked like clones of each other, save for the Greek letters and color scheme that adorned them. The night was exhausting, having to make the same small talk over and over again at each party, something I was far from skilled at. The parties and girls all blended together and I could barely distinguish them from each other. But I somehow survived all seven parties, my voice hoarse from yelling to be heard over all the other people.

A few days after the first round ended, I went to meet my rush adviser, a senior in one of the sororities, in the common room of the Women's Building, where dozens of advisers and rushees sat scattered across the floor.

As I waited to speak to my adviser, I fidgeted with my jacket zipper. *Did any of the girls like me? Will all the sororities cut me? Will I make it to the next round?*

Then she called my name, and I followed her to a small open space on the floor between other people. We sat on the floor, cross-legged, facing each other.

"Okay, as you know, each sorority has to cut some girls after the first round. I've got your results." As she sifted through her paperwork, my stomach turned. "So, I have some great news for you—you were invited back to round two by all seven sororities!"

"Oh, wow. I wasn't, um, expecting that." I couldn't stop a big smile from spreading across my face.

"Yep, you should feel really great—this means all the sororities liked you. And since you were invited back to round two by all seven sororities and there are only six parties in round two, you'll have to eliminate one of the sororities. You need to decide which one you are going to drop."

As I walked back to my dorm in a daze, conflicting feelings of confusion, hope, fear, and excitement swirled together like vibrant colors in a kaleidoscope. *After years of moving from one high school to another, and never finding a feeling of belonging, could I actually finally belong somewhere?* I didn't want to get my hopes up too much, but I couldn't help imagining what it might feel like to be part of a group of popular girls. I had never felt like anything but an outsider at school.

Round two parties happened the next weekend. This time there were only six parties, they were longer, and we were told to dress more formally. I left round two emotionally exhausted from trying to impress people—all the while feeling like none of them would have ever so much as talked to me in high school.

A few days after round two ended, I had to meet with my rush adviser again. As I waited in the common room, I saw a few girls scurrying out of the room with mascara running down their face. My insecurities intensified as I waited to hear if I had been invited back for round three parties.

As luck would have it, I was invited back to four round three parties! *Is this a mistake? Is there another "Kristin Griffith"?*

Round three parties were held the next weekend and this time the dress code was even more formal. I couldn't help but notice I was probably the only rushee not wearing a skirt or dress. I was saving my one skirt in case I got invited to the fourth and final round of parties.

A few days later, I stopped in the restroom in the Women's Building before my appointment with my rush adviser and heard two different girls in the bathroom stalls crying. I stopped cold as I realized they had probably just heard from their rush adviser that they were cut from rush—no sororities had invited them back for the last round. They would not be getting a bid from a sorority.

While I signed up for rush not sure I would want to be in a sorority and thinking I had an extremely slim chance of getting accepted,

I now felt differently. Being invited back to parties had made me start to believe that maybe they did like me, at least a little. *Maybe I'm not as awkward as I think. Maybe confident, cool girls could like me. Maybe I could fit in with them.* At the parties, the women seemed to be truly interested in what I was saying. This was an unfamiliar, but amazing, feeling. I found myself now desperately longing to be part of it all.

I heard my adviser call my name and felt myself holding my breath as I walked to hear whether I had been invited to any final round parties.

2

BID DROPPING

January, Freshman Year

A week after round three parties, excitement and apprehension propelled me on the pathways across campus. Alpha Chi Omega and Kappa Alpha Theta had invited me to their fourth and final round of parties. After these formal parties, sororities would make final decisions about who to cut and who to extend bids to. We had been warned that even if you had made it to round four without being cut, a number of rushees would not receive any bids after the formal parties. And, for those that did receive a bid, it was often not from their first choice of a sorority—so we had to be prepared. If I were cut, then my hopes of joining a sorority would be over.

When I entered the formal Theta party for the final round of rush, I felt very self-conscious. Most of the rushees and the Thetas wore long, formal black dresses, with glamorous makeup, jewelry, and hair. I forced myself to wear my one skirt—a black and white houndstooth print miniskirt that was very tight now. All the pizza and fried mozzarella sticks had gone straight to my ass. A Peanuts

Band-Aid covered a scrape on my knee from an intramural soccer game. I wore my generic wire-framed glasses, as I couldn't see without them. I heard my sister's voice in my head: "Dork!"

After round three, I knew without a doubt that Theta was my first choice. As a couple of Thetas greeted me at the door, my longing to be accepted propelled me to fight through my awkwardness. Streamers and balloons of black and gold packed the expansive room; vases filled with black and gold pansies were arranged on black tablecloths, along with gold confetti.

A long table held hors d'oeuvres and a massive silver chocolate fountain. I picked up a strawberry with a long toothpick, held it under the fountain, and let the creamy milk chocolate cover it. I took a bite, trying my best not to get chocolate on my face.

I recognized a few Thetas from previous parties and two girls from Theta who played on my intramural soccer team found me in the crowd. We talked about our last game and my knee injury. A constant stream of girls kept coming by to talk to me as well. My conversations with these girls had been more substantial than any I'd ever had with girls prior to college. All the attention gave me a feeling of acceptance that felt both comforting and exciting.

About halfway through the party, about 75 Thetas and 30 rushees gathered around the piano as a girl dressed as a black cat began playing the song "Memory" from the musical *Cats*. The initials for Theta were KAT. More cat girls emerged from behind a wall in the now dimly lit room, slinking out in sequined black spandex, fuzzy black ears, long tails bobbing. One girl began to sing, and others chimed in, crawling and twirling. I was mesmerized by the feminine grace and exquisite voices of the Theta girls.

After the party ended, girls I had met hugged me goodbye, one after another. I hadn't received so many hugs in my entire life. In high school I used to watch girls hug each other and envied their relationships. My parents still joke about the time in middle school when I tried to shake my sister's hand after opening a Christmas gift she gave me. More girl bonding had occurred for me during sorority rush than in my whole life up to that point. Girls asked me questions and seemed to really want to know the answers. They laughed at my stories. They seemed intrigued. This group of talented, pretty, smart women listened to me and kept inviting me back.

As I left the Theta party, I momentarily forgot that I was "Four Eyes". I wondered if this was what it was like to feel popular.

It was about ten degrees out, with wind chill, but warmth radiated from my whole being and I couldn't stop smiling.

Saturday morning, a week after the round four Kappa Alpha Theta and Alpha Chi Omega formal parties I attended, I sat staring at the beige phone on my desk. About a third of all the freshman girls across campus were doing the same.

It was almost nine am. I heard the ticking of my watch's second hand and the heater groaned as the warm air ratcheted up. I normally played a CD on my boom box in the mornings, but this morning I didn't dare: I needed to hear my phone. Luckily, my roommate had been gone all night, probably hooking up with a random guy, as usual.

My foot tapped the floor. I chewed on my fingernails, staring at the phone. A few days before, my rush adviser had explained that if a sorority didn't select me, I would receive a call with the bad news, so I'd know not to come to the bid dropping ceremony later in the day.

Please don't ring. Please don't ring. Please don't ring.

Normally, at this time of morning on the weekend, everyone was asleep and the dorms were quiet. I thought I heard a phone ring down the hall. A few minutes later I heard someone storm down the hall, crying—I was sure it was a rushee who'd gotten a call from her adviser saying she didn't get a bid and not to come to the bid dropping ceremony.

My heart pounded faster. *Please let me get a bid. Please let me get a bid. Please let me get a bid.* My watch went *tick tock, tick tock, tick tock.*

At 9:50 a.m., I thought I heard another girl crying. *Only 10 minutes left. In 10 minutes I'll know.* I stared at my watch. I watched the second hand slowly pass by each number.

Tick tock, tick tock, tick tock.

The minute hand finally reached 10 a.m. I stared at the phone in disbelief. *Could it be a mistake? Would I get to the bid dropping ceremony and they'd say they called me, but they had my number wrong?*

My heart began to slow down a little and a sigh of relief escaped my body. *Will I get a bid from Alpha Chi Omega or Kappa Alpha Theta?* I remembered the red decorations from the AXΩ formal party, the black and gold of the KAΘ party.

Please let me get a bid from Theta. I really want a bid from Theta.

I tried to keep busy as I waited for the bid dropping ceremony that afternoon. I showered and got some breakfast with my boyfriend of a couple of months, William, and a few others from my dorm.

I met William in our first semester of freshman year, because a few of us from our floor spent hours almost every day playing card games in his dorm room. William was a clean-cut, shy pre-med student from Illinois. It was a miracle he went out with me at all after the most embarrassing moment of my life happened right before we started dating.

One night, I came back from a frat party drunk and knocked on William's door. I didn't want to go back to my room because I was avoiding my roommate. William let me sleep on his bed with him. I fell asleep on top of his blue-and-white-striped comforter.

After I left William's room in the morning, I went to the restroom and discovered that blood had leaked out of my tampon and through my jean shorts! I was horrified. *What if it got on William's comforter?*

I avoided William the rest of that day, mortified. That night, as I walked into the dorm, near the laundry rooms, I saw William taking his comforter out of the washing machine and putting it in to the dryer! Despite this mishap, we miraculously started dating shortly before winter break.

All throughout breakfast, I could think of nothing but the upcoming bid dropping ceremony. *If I receive a bid from Alpha Chi Omega, will I accept it? The girls are nice there, but the Kappa Alpha Thetas are just so cool, charismatic, and confident. I feel like I really connected with them.* I was afraid to even hope that I'd been accepted by them.

Finally, Becky and I walked to the nondenominational chapel in the center of campus, surrounded by hundreds of other freshman girls all going the same place. Anxious energy surrounded us. Sorority girls with Greek letters on their shirts greeted us and told us to take a seat on the left side of the chapel with the rest of the rushees.

Inside, light streamed into the high ceilings through the

multicolored stained-glass windows. We sat in the first empty seats, about 10 rows from the back, with hundreds of other wide-eyed girls. On the right were about a hundred sorority girls, Greek letters across their chests combining with the colored light from the window created a complex pattern of pink, red, yellow, blue, and purple. While our side was quiet and tense, the right side was more boisterous, the sorority girls hugging each other and chatting.

Then a hush swept through the chapel. A dozen sorority girls stood in front of the pulpit. One welcomed us and explained what was going to happen. "When we call your name, you will come up here and we'll hand you an envelope that contains your bid from a sorority. Do not open it yet. Once everyone has their envelope, I will instruct all rushees to open their bids at once. After you open your bid, find a member of that sorority. You will then go to that sorority suite for the afternoon and evening, where they have special activities planned. Have fun, everyone, and congratulations! Many girls did not make it this far, but all of you were hand-selected by a sorority. That means they think you will fit right in and they would love to have you join them as a pledge! Okay, so let's get started."

A sorority girl at the pulpit started calling names, alphabetically. Each name reverberated in the chapel, almost visible in the air. A steady stream of girls walked to the front.

When I finally heard her call "Kristin Griffith," I squeezed out of my row, almost tripping in my nervousness. I walked up the aisle to the front, where a sorority girl hugged me and congratulated me. Then another girl handed me a thick cream-colored envelope—as rich and formal as a wedding invitation.

Those of us with envelopes fidgeted with them in our seats. *Please let it say Theta. Please let it say Theta. Please let it say*

Theta. Name after name after name was called, creating a sea of rushees fixated on the envelopes in their laps.

Finally, all the bids had been given out. The girl at the front announced, "We are going to count down from three and when I get to one, you may open your envelopes. Ready, everyone?"

We all stared at the envelopes in our hands, ready to tear into them.

"Three…two…one. You may now open your bids!"

In a shuffling flurry, we all ripped our envelopes open. I pulled out the thick luxurious paper inside. On the top was a black and gold seal, and in fancy lettering it read, "We, the members of Kappa Alpha Theta invite you, Kristin Heather Griffith, to become a member of our chapter, Alpha Iota, on the 20th day of January, 1992."

Excitement rushed through my body—like when I scored a goal in soccer, but better. I smiled ear to ear.

Becky looked at me and said "Theta?"

I said, "Yes, Theta!"

"Me too!" she said. We hugged.

Most of the girls around me were hugging, but some looked disappointed—they obviously had not gotten their first choice. A group of Thetas found us and whisked us away from the chapel to the Theta suite. When we arrived, the remaining Thetas welcomed us with singing, clapping, and more hugging. They presented us all with identical white T-shirts adorned with kites and KAPPA ALPHA THETA PLEDGE CLASS 1992. We all put our new shirts on and a Theta snapped pictures of us. I couldn't have wiped the huge grin from my face if I'd tried.

Then we all crammed into cars and headed to Chuck E. Cheese. Members from one of the fraternities on campus joined us there for an evening of pizza, video games, and Skee-Ball.

Finally, I felt like I might belong somewhere. But my place wasn't guaranteed. I would still have to make it through pledging. What I would need to do to become a full-fledged sorority member, and how many of us would make that final cut, was a mystery to me.

3

PLEDGING

February, Freshman Year

Rumors were circulating that Pi Beta Phi hazed their pledges on the roof of the library, forcing them to undress to only their panties and bras. Then, sorority members circled all the areas of fat on each girl's body with black Sharpie. They made the pledges stand there in the cold and made fun of all their imperfections until they cried. This was just one of many stories I heard.

When pledging started, our Theta pledge chair said there would be no hazing, and gave us a number to call if we ever felt we'd been treated poorly. I had heard of fraternity pledges dying from being forced to drink too much alcohol. Fear mixed with excitement swirled in my head as I wondered what was really in store for me during pledging. We didn't know how many of us would get cut and not be initiated as a full-fledged member of Theta.

Early in the pledge period, we arrived at Becky's parents' house in the St. Louis suburbs for a pledge retreat—the same Becky that had convinced me to rush. As Becky was the only pledge from St.

Louis, her house was the natural choice.

One of the rooms was cleared of furniture to make room for the 30 pledges to sit in a circle on the beige carpet. We passed around pizza boxes, paper plates, and paper napkins. After most of us had finished eating, Becky explained that we were going to get to know each other.

I learned that my pledge sisters came from a variety of places: California, Nebraska, New York, Boston, South Carolina, a rural town in Texas, and lots from the East Coast. Many were pre-med, but there was a range from art to business to architecture to engineering to psychology.

By the end of the evening there had been crying, laughing, and hugs all around while we shared personal stories of our lives before college. It was now late, and I changed into flannel pajama pants and a T-shirt. We laid out our sleeping bags and pillows in the big main room and some of the adjoining rooms. I snuggled into my cozy sleeping bag as the talking died down to whispers and giggles. I could feel the warmth and closeness in the room. I had always longed to be a part of a group like this.

During the pledge period, I was distracted by my complicated relationship with William, my boyfriend, and Jake in the Hat. Jake in the Hat acquired his nickname to distinguish him from the other guy on his freshman dorm floor named Jake. Jake in the Hat always wore a brown fedora—way before Justin Timberlake made it cool. The other was called Jake in the Box, because one night he got really drunk and sat inside a cardboard box and wouldn't come out. It was quite some time before he eventually emerged.

Jake in the Hat was six feet tall and looked like a surfer dude, though his hometown was Shaker Heights, Ohio. He rowed on the crew team at Wash U and also had played soccer in high school, like me.

Peppermint Schnapps facilitated my first interaction with Jake in the Hat, months before William and I started dating. We sat on a bed in someone's dorm room, early freshman year, along with some others, drinking and talking. I was still a newbie at drinking as I had gotten drunk for the first time just a few weeks earlier on wine coolers. Immediately discovering that alcohol reduced my social anxiety set me on a path to frequent drinking, which would get me in trouble throughout college.

All the lights in the room were off, but the dorm door was open, with some dim red lighting creeping in from the hallway. Jake in the Hat gulped from the large bottle of peppermint Schnapps and handed it to me. "Want some?" he asked.

I sniffed it. The smell of peppermint and hard liquor burned my nose, and I shuddered. With the abandon only a clueless freshman can have, I downed a mouthful of the clear liquid. The hot peppermint fumes filled my chest. We passed the bottle around the room and everyone drank from it. After a number of swigs, the bed began to rotate slowly. Jake in the Hat kissed me with lips of wet mint. My hazy head wobbled, but we kept kissing and kissing, our tongues swirling inside each other's mouths.

We stumbled down the dimly lit hallway to my room. I tried to gingerly knock on my closed door, but my drunken efforts produced a loud bang as I stumbled inside. Madison wasn't home, luckily.

Jake in the Hat and I fell into my single bed and continued making out, then quickly passed out. I awoke in the morning to a jackhammer drilling into my head and climbed out of my cramped position, squished between the wall and Jake in the Hat, to use the restroom. That's how it all began.

After that, he started stopping by my dorm floor almost every day. He joined us in William and Fred's room and hung out while we played cards, even after William and I had started dating.

• • •

Jake in the Hat pledged the Kappa Sigma fraternity first semester freshman year and invited me to one of their dances. It made me feel like I was part of the "in" crowd—something I had never thought I would feel or be. I wore the same dress I had worn to senior prom. The black satiny skirt landed right below my knees, and the top was fitted, with spaghetti straps. I wore white satin heels from Payless. The dress and heels made me feel like I was dressing in drag, but that was the uniform expected of me. Jake in the Hat wore a traditional black tuxedo and brought me a burgundy corsage to wear around my wrist. In a picture snapped in my dorm room before we left, we stood in front of my messy desk and New Order poster. He looked like a rock star with long, white-blond wavy hair (no hat) and a serious smirk.

We walked across campus to the Kappa Sigma frat house. The warm and bright house was filled with guys in suits and girls in dresses. I had only seen the frat house packed at late-night parties; it looked completely different at 4 p.m. Fraternity pictures from years past lined the walls; each guy looked almost identical. It reminded me of military lines, guys with formulaic haircuts, shaved of their personalities.

Finally, we headed for the buses. It would take about 45 minutes to get to the hotel downtown where the dance was. About 100 of us took over the brick pathway that led down frat row, past frat houses adorned with Greek letters and guys lounging on couches in the yard or smoking on the front steps, Pearl Jam blaring.

Past the last house there were about 500 steps that led down to the parking area where the buses waited. This was the first time I had worn heels freshman year. Dresses and heels and other girly stuff weren't my thing—I had always been a tomboy. I tried makeup once, in seventh grade, at the urging of a friend. I grabbed the mirror with my left hand, closed my right eye, and awkwardly tried drawing on my eyelid with the brush. After applying eyeshadow to my other eye and blush to my cheeks, I looked at myself in the mirror and saw someone that wasn't me. Immediately I had the urge to wipe it off.

My mom worried that I was too much of a tomboy, as early as elementary school. I played tackle football with the boys in the neighborhood almost every day—often past when the street-lights came on. Despite chipping a tooth after being tackled on the sidewalk, I was committed to the thought of becoming a Dallas Cowboys football player when I grew up. On the other hand, my sister wanted to be a Dallas Cowboys cheerleader, like many young girls in Dallas.

My mom mistakenly bought me a few Barbie dolls when I was in elementary school. She later told me she had found the bodies with the heads missing, so she stopped buying them and acquiesced to my requests for Star Wars figurines. My sister and I liked to play my parents' Star Wars eight-track tape while I pretended to be Luke Skywalker and my sister was Princess Leia.

By the end of sixth grade, I attempted to hide the more-boyish part of myself. I tried carrying a purse in junior high, but it never felt right. I hid it in my room after a few weeks so my mom wouldn't ask why I wasn't using it. I wore dresses to the formal dances so I wouldn't be the only girl not in a dress, but nowhere else. I fought my mom on this many times. Although I had very short hair when I was young and people sometimes mistook me for a boy, by the end of elementary school I'd grown my blond hair long, and I kept it that way into college. I never liked my long hair, but felt pressure to look like everyone else—up till then, I'd never seen a girl my age with short hair.

By college, I was still a tomboy at heart but trying to hide it the best I could. I held onto the railing as I unsteadily wobbled down the stairs in my heels. Now, these were not eight-inch stilettos—they were probably only two-inch heels. Not difficult for most girls, but for me a real challenge. I may have been able to dive and catch a football, but heels were a different beast altogether.

We climbed on the bus and immediately the guys started shouting. "Hey dude, pass me a beer!" In the back of the bus, there were a bunch of huge coolers. "Anyone else want one?"

"Yeah, fagatron, pass me two." The term "fagatron" was constantly thrown around by frat guys; by this point it barely registered because I had heard it so much.

"Is there any hard liquor?"

"Yeah, there's JD and rum and vodka."

"Pass me the JD. Who wants to do shots?"

The guys started cheering and yelling, while the girls mostly sat quietly next to their dates. Guys started passing the bottles of hard liquor around, chugging from the bottles and shaming whoever didn't want any. Burps echoed around the bus, followed by a few cheers from the guys.

We arrived at a fancy hotel in downtown St. Louis, disembarked, and passed through an ornate lobby filled with red and gold rugs and gold chandeliers. We walked directly to the long line at the bar. Drinks were free and unlimited. We grabbed plates and moved through the buffet line, then sat next to a few members of Jake's pledge class and their dates, at a white linen–covered table.

When the music came on, I joined a few women I recognized from the dorm to dance in the large ballroom. I barely felt a buzz. The drinks were very watered-down. I couldn't fit enough drinks in my bladder to get drunk.

After dancing for hours while Jake in the Hat hung out with his pledge brothers, we took the bus back to the Kappa Sigma house. Jake in the Hat walked me back to my dorm room at about 1 a.m. Luckily my roommate wasn't there. We moved to my bed and I turned on Enigma, my hookup mood music.

"Wanna have sex?" he asked me.

"Okay." I was still a virgin. I never stressed about being a virgin or losing my virginity, though. I didn't have strong feelings about sex either way, but was curious.

With little fanfare, we had missionary-style sex that was fine— nothing earth-shattering, but okay. I felt a bit cooler afterward. More experienced. More grown-up. Like I was now part of the club. However, sex wasn't nearly as exciting as I thought it might be, considering what a big deal people made of it. It felt just mildly interesting.

One typical Thursday night while I was pledging, I met some of my fellow pledges at the Rat, a bar on campus, for drinks. William didn't join us because he hated the Thursday night scene, mostly overrun with frat boys and sorority girls.

After the band finished, my sisters and I moved over to the Kappa Sigma fraternity house for their weekly Thursday after party. The couches were cleared from the living room and hordes of people danced drunkenly. At some point, Jake in the Hat, now a member of Kappa Sig, spotted me and joined us. One thing led to another and we ended up downstairs in the large, empty kitchen. Industrial-size pots and pans hung from the ceiling and shiny stainless steel covered almost every surface. In our drunken state we attacked each other with clumsy groping and kisses.

The next night, Jake in the Hat, William, William's roommate, Fred, myself, and a few other friends from the floor were getting into a car and Fred said to Jake in the Hat, "Did someone hit you with a baseball bat? What's up with all those hickeys on your neck?" Jake's neck was completely covered in pink hickeys. Although he was wearing a turtleneck, you could still see them peeking out.

Jake in the Hat said "Oh, it's nothing" and quickly jumped into the car.

Fred shot me a steely look in the dark. William didn't visibly react. Although William knew Jake in the Hat and I had hooked up before we started dating, I don't know if he suspected we had afterward too, and if his polite and agreeable personality prevented him from ever mentioning it.

• • •

On the morning of Valentine's Day, I heard my door creaking open. I slowly and carefully rolled over in bed, trying not to disturb Jake in the Hat. My head throbbed from my hangover.

William had just placed a box of chocolates and bouquet of long-stemmed red roses on my desk near the door. He looked at me and left without saying anything, closing the door quietly behind him.

I dragged my tired, hungover body up. Jake in the Hat left, and I walked to Bear's Den and ate some greasy pizza to soak up the remaining alcohol.

By the afternoon I was feeling a little better. I walked across my dorm hall to William's room. The door was slightly ajar. I knocked softly.

William sat on the top of his comforter, leaning against the wall with a textbook open and a notebook open beside him.

"Hey," I said.

"Hey."

I stepped halfway in the room. "So, I wanted to thank you for the candy and flowers. It was very sweet of you."

"You are welcome." William's face looked serious, his body language stiff.

"Um, so I just wanted to explain why Jake was there. I know it probably seemed weird he was in my bed."

"Yeah."

"So, what happened was that Jake came by last night because he was really stressed out. He came by to talk. We talked for a while. I was kinda drunk and at some point fell asleep. I guess he passed out and fell asleep in my bed too. I didn't realize it until you came in this morning. I just wanted you to know that all we did was talk and that nothing happened."

William stared at me, his textbook still in his lap. "Okay."

"I'm sorry. I know it looked bad." Still standing awkwardly by the door, I said, "I guess I should go. I should get some studying done."

He didn't say anything else or move a muscle.

I continued, "Okay, well, I guess I'll see you later then?"

"Yep."

I had lied. I had failed to mention the part where Jake in the Hat and I got naked and fooled around. I only felt mildly guilty, though; I blamed it on the alcohol and the fact that William and I barely had a sexual relationship—not much more than kissing going on. I never told William and I'm still not sure if William ever knew that Jake in the Hat and I sometimes had drunken hookups while we were dating.

During one of our pledge meetings, one of the pledge leaders explained that we would each have a pledge mom, one of the active members. The purpose of a pledge mom is to guide new members through pledging and, possibly, initiation. We ranked our top three choices and all the actives listed pledges they were interested in being a mom to, then we were matched up. I chose three of the actives that I'd had more in-depth conversations with during rush and to whom I felt a connection. We would soon be kicking off pledge mom week, during which our pledge mom would give us clues about her identity. Then, during initiation, assuming we made it that far, we'd find out who she was.

The first morning of that week, I stepped out of my dorm room to find pink construction paper completely covering the outside of my door. Bold multicolored letters spelled KRISTIN, with pieces of wrapped candy, cut-out hearts, kites, and envelopes taped all over. I opened one of the envelopes and pulled out a piece of paper inside, which said, "I am from New Jersey." Other envelopes said, "I'm a sophomore" and "I have long blond hair."

Seeing my door decorated reminded me of how at my high school in Austin, the popular senior girls would decorate the varsity football players' lockers every Friday they had a game. Red, white, and blue streamers waved as students passed by; the player's names shone in bubbly letters. The football players stood near their lockers on game day beaming with pride, strutting through the halls wearing matching team gear as if they owned the school, while I walked by unnoticed. I felt now what it was like to be wanted, liked, accepted. I bounced to class that day, sucking on one of the pieces of candy from the door.

Another day, the actives instructed the pledges to come to the sorority suite during lunch for a special surprise from our secret pledge mom. One of my pledge sisters explained that I was supposed to find an envelope with my name on it, then follow the clues for a scavenger hunt.

I looked around the crowded suite. Dozens of wrapped presents, balloons, and decorated shoeboxes were scattered everywhere. High-pitched squeals erupted every few minutes.

I found an envelope with my name on it. A clue sat inside. For every clue I solved I found a gift, a clue about the identity of my pledge mom, and another clue. There were five clues in all, each inside a balloon I had to pop to get the clue on a little piece of paper inside. *Pop!* "Sorry!" I said as girls nearby jumped.

I came away with a little stuffed animal and some candy, but no closer to figuring out who my pledge mom was. As soon as I thought I knew, another clue would point in a different direction.

Late one night, after dinner, the actives told us all to meet at one of the fraternity houses. As I walked in, all the guys were standing on and around the staircase leading up to the second floor. I joined some of the other pledges at the bottom of the stairwell. The frat guys pulled one of our pledges to the front and serenaded her with "Brown Eyed Girl." Then one of the guys said that the serenade was from her pledge mom.

Toward the end of that week, a note on my door said to be in my room at 8 p.m. on Thursday night. At 8, a clean-cut guy sheepishly knocked on my open door. "Hi, I'm Tom. I'm a friend of your pledge mom. Can I come in?"

He then awkwardly walked into my room. "I've brought you milk and cookies and am going to read you a bedtime story." He handed me a carton of milk and two massive chocolate chip cookies. The soft cookie melted in my mouth. I washed it down with a sip of cold milk.

He smiled at me shyly and showed me the cover of the book: *The Little Engine That Could.* "Your pledge mom picked this book with you in mind."

He read the first page, then showed me the pictures before turning to the next page. I continued to eat my cookie and drink my milk. He read, "As the little train tried to pull another train that had broken down to the top of the hill, the little train said 'I think I can. I think I can. I think I can. I know I can.'"

Tom finished the story and closed the book, then handed it to me. As he got up to leave, he said, "Look inside—your pledge mom has left another clue for you."

I read the clue, but still wasn't sure who my pledge mom was.

During the pledge period, the actives gave us a Kappa Alpha Theta Pledge Book titled "Theta for a Lifetime." They told us we needed to memorize all 49 pages of it, because we would need to pass an exam in order to be eligible to be a full-fledged sorority member. It contained information on KAΘ's history, rules, behavior standards, responsibilities as a member, dues, symbols, etc. We all spent hours studying together in the sorority suite and learned things like the Greek alphabet, official colors (black and gold), our sorority flower (black and gold pansy), symbol (kite), secret whistle, secret handshake, the founders' history, sorority songs, and the chapter meeting opening rituals. I took the test and then anxiously waited for the results. I couldn't stand the thought of making it this far, only to be cut now.

4

INITIATION

March, Freshman Year

On March 1, 1992, all Theta pledges and actives met at a three-story red-brick house on the edge of campus. Inside, a Theta handed me a black robe and said to change into it.

Once everyone in my pledge class had changed into identical black robes, we were all blindfolded. After a few minutes, someone touched my upper arm and whispered, "I'm going to lead you to the ceremony now. Just trust me."

My heart raced as I walked, sure I would run into something. The grip tightened slightly, and my leader said, "Stop. Hold for a second."

I stopped. I could hear whispering and feet shuffling. Then she guided me down the stairs. The cold metal of the railing made me shiver. I cautiously slid my foot down each stair, one by one. Finally, my sister said, "Okay, one more step."

We continued. The floor was cold beneath my socked feet.

She said, "Okay, there's a cushion right in front of you. You're going to kneel down on it."

I carefully knelt down and felt a soft cushion underneath. I heard a voice from far away say, "Okay, Thetas, you now may remove the pledges' blindfolds and the initiation ceremony will begin."

My sister's fingers untied the knot at the back of my head, and I opened my eyes. The dark room was illuminated by dozens of white candles at the front of the room. All of us pledges were on our knees on cushions, in rows at the back of the room. The actives surrounded us, wearing the same black robes.

One by one, actives led us to the front of the room. When I got to the front, an active asked me to chant a few sentences of commitment to Kappa Alpha Theta. A sister handed me a massive gold chalice, which I held in two hands.

"Take a sip to seal your lifelong commitment to Theta," she said.

I tipped the chalice. The dark liquid tasted like tart grape juice.

The sister then pinned a black, gold, and white kite-shaped pin with the Kappa Alpha Theta sorority crest onto my robe. I was now officially a member of Theta. I couldn't hold back my grin.

After the ceremony, my pledge mom, Adrienne, presented me with my first set of letters: a vibrant red KAΘ sewn on a black T-shirt. Then, I was given a hand-assembled initiation booklet with notes from all the actives. Mine started with, "HEY CRUNCHY WOMAN! WELCOME TO THETA!!" I flipped through the pages and pages of notes of congratulations and inspirational quotes from all the Theta women.

"We are so glad to have you as one of our pledges. You're so cute!!" "Being independent is great, but a little help once in a while is also okay. Remember, your Theta sisters will always be here for you." "If you let it, Theta can give you more than you ever imagined. Welcome to sisterhood!"

My new pledge mom also gave me a handmade "family tree": a construction paper tree with my name written at the top. The names of the rest of my lineage were handwritten on the tree trunk. My body filled with warmth as I took in my new Theta family.

At the same time, I was struggling with my roommate, Madison. One night I lay alone in bed. I was listening to a Pet Shop Boys CD on my boom box, nestled under my blanket, excited to get a full night's sleep before class in the morning. Then, I suddenly heard two loud voices outside my room. The doorknob turned, and Madison and some random guy barged in, talking loudly and turning on the light. They were obviously drunk, stumbling around. The guy saw me and said "Uh, hi" then turned back to Madison, who pretended I wasn't there.

I kept my eyes closed, willing it to end soon. Madison grabbed her toiletries bag and some pink frilly outfit to wear to bed and left. It sounded like he was undressing, just a few feet away from me. I peeked just in time to see him jump in Madison's bed in boxers and a T-shirt. *Ugh, he's going to stay.* It was too late for me to find someone to crash with.

As I was contemplating my fate, Madison came back in, turned off the light, and jumped in bed with this guy. My music was still going, on repeat. Their whispers were muffled. There was a little rustling around, then silence. At some point I fell asleep.

I awoke to groaning, opened my eyes slowly, and could see their shadows moving in the dark. They were having sex.

What do I do now? Do I confront them or just pretend to be asleep and wait for it to be over? If I had been my sister, who was always bold, I would have yelled at them and told them to get out. But I was me, who hates confrontation, so I closed my eyes, tried not to listen, and hoped that it would end soon. I tried not to move a muscle, so they wouldn't know I was awake—almost afraid to breathe for fear they could hear me. I tried focusing on the music, but all I could think of was how much I disliked her and wished I had a different roommate. She was awful and inconsiderate and didn't care about anyone but herself.

At some point there were some groans, the rustling slowed and then stopped, and there was a little whispering, then quiet.

I decided to go to my resident adviser to ask if I could switch roommates. He said that part of the college experience was about learning to get along with people who are very different from you, so the answer was no.

I started to cry. Everything felt overwhelming. My sister had just gotten out of rehab, but there was no telling how long her sobriety would last. We had a very strained relationship, and I was worried sick that she might overdose. There was nothing I could do from 800 miles away.

My RA suggested I go to the Student Counseling Center and make an appointment to talk to someone. I set up a session, which became the first of many throughout all four years of college.

5

SPRING FORMAL

April, Freshman Year

I entered the same big lecture hall on campus that I had gone to every Sunday night since initiation. Attendance at chapter meetings was required for all Thetas. The officers sat behind a long desk at the front of the hall.

As usual, the meeting opened with a short verse from the Bible that we all recited together. It always made me cringe a little since I didn't believe in God. My parents were atheists, where science and proof ruled.

Every day when my elementary school classmates and I got to "one nation under God" in the Pledge of Allegiance, I squirmed in my seat and barely whispered that part. In high school, my grandmother had given me a Bible with my name engraved on it. I decided to try reading it and to use a yellow highlighter to mark every passage that didn't make sense from a scientific standpoint: the Red Sea parting, a woman made from the rib of a man, for starters. I only got through a few chapters.

The meeting started with our Formal Chair standing up and shouting, "Is everyone excited for formal this year?!" Everyone snapped their fingers and there were a few "woo-hoo"s.

Our formal chair continued, telling us that the formal would be held at a very fancy hotel a few hours away. There would be a buffet dinner and an open bar, and we'd all stay overnight in the hotel. "It's going to be the best formal yet!"

She paused. The snapping of fingers resumed. Her long hair bounced as she talked.

"Okay, so you need to find a date! Bring your boyfriend or a guy you're interested in. Or reach out to us and we can set you up with an awesome guy! Next, make sure you've got a formal dress and that your date rents a tux or wears a suit. That's all for now. Can't wait!"

The message was clear: a guy was the only acceptable date. There was no acknowledgment of or space for anything outside that.

• • •

Back in my dorm, I walked across the hall to William and Fred's room. The door stood ajar and I could hear cheery voices from inside. I poked my head in. "Hey, guys!"

William, Fred, and Zion sat on the floor in the middle of the room. On William's side of the room, the bed was made, CDs of bands like Erasure and Tori Amos were neatly organized. His dark brown hair was neatly styled, and he wore crisp dark Levi's, a fresh button-down polo shirt, and loafers.

Fred's shaggy blond hair, oversized T-shirt, and soccer shorts stood in sharp contrast. Zion, a tall Asian guy with a mustache and long, silky black hair, lived down the hall.

Fred said, "Hey! Join us! Now that we have four people, we can play euchre."

I sat next to them. An open bag of tortilla chips and a big jar of salsa sat on the floor. Fred grabbed a chip and dunked it into the salsa. I followed suit.

Fred said, "Okay, you and William on one team!" He winked at us. "Zion and me on the other."

William and I had been dating for about five months at this point, even though we hadn't even come close to having sex. William moved so that he sat opposite from me, smiling. Fred dealt the cards. Laughter and high fives filled the room as we played.

At some point we ordered pizzas. A few minutes later, Jake in the Hat walked in with a swagger. "Hey, what's up?" He plopped down on Fred's bed and gave me a sly sideways smile. I looked at William, who was busy shuffling cards, then smiled back at Jake in the Hat. My face began to flush as Fred shot me a look.

After a few more hours of cards, I said, "Hey guys, I should head to bed." I looked at William and said, "Can we talk a minute in private?"

We walked out and down to the end of the hallway. It was past 2 a.m. and the lights were dim. Not a soul was in sight. I sat down against a wall and William sat next to me. I could smell his cologne, Colors by Benetton.

Despite my on-again, off-again interactions with Jake in the Hat, I charged ahead. "So, I've got something to ask you. The Theta spring formal is coming up and I wanted to know if you'd be my date?"

"Sure."

He gave me a quick peck on the lips, and we hugged.

William and I checked in to the hotel and changed. He looked debonair in his classic black tuxedo and black-and-white houndstooth bowtie and cummerbund. I wore the same black and white dress I'd worn to my high school prom and Jake in the Hat's fraternity dance.

We entered a huge ballroom with dozens of circular tables covered with white tablecloths and massive crystal chandeliers. Music blared from the DJ. Lines hovered around the buffet and bar. We ate before grabbing a drink and hitting the dance floor.

We danced to '80s and '90s music for hours, grabbing a few drinks along the way. William was, hands down, the best guy dancer there. He danced with attitude, snapping his head to the right and left, moving to the beat, and holding on to his belt, oozing confidence and ease. The majority of the other guys did the white guy stiff-foot-back-and-forth-shuffle with a look of severe discomfort on their faces. A few guys made off-beat running-man-like jerky movements with a goofy grin. They looked like they were thinking, "I am such a good dancer. Everyone, look at me!"

At the end of the night, William and I headed back to our room. Although hazy from all the alcohol, something still didn't feel quite right.

William had seen me at my best and at my worst freshman year. During the best moments we talked for hours about everything and nothing after everyone had gone to sleep. In December, right before the holiday break, our group of friends got together for a Christmas and Hanukkah celebration. We turned off the dorm lights, and the bright lights twinkled on the tree, with many colorful wrapped gifts underneath. We felt festive and full of laughter. William gave me lingerie, and everyone oohed and aahed. The gift shocked me given we rarely fooled around. I don't remember ever wearing it. By the time Spring Formal rolled around, we had still never had sex.

At my worst, William had to deal with my drinking.

There was a rule in our dorm that if you drank too much, puked in the dorm, and someone else had to clean it up, you had to pay that person $50. Although my puke was cleaned up at least five times freshman year, primarily by William, I never had to pay anyone. Once, William told me I drank so much in their room that I fell face first into Fred's closet, and then when I got across the hall to my dorm room I took the big gallon jug of Bacardi rum from the top of my closet and started drinking out of it. Other times I blacked out for at least a portion of the night. I had discovered that alcohol helped me be less shy and self-conscious, but I usually took it way too far and couldn't easily control it.

So, when William and I got back to our hotel room, before we even had a chance to change, I broke up with him. I said we'd be better off as friends. I don't remember it being premeditated; it was an impulsive decision. But I do remember my relief afterward, like a weight had been lifted.

6

THURTENE CARNIVAL

May, Freshman Year

Our last big sorority event of the year was Thurtene, a massive carnival put on by Wash U students. A huge parking lot on campus was filled with a Ferris wheel, roller coasters for kids, and other carnival rides, along with booths selling hot dogs, funnel cakes, and burgers. Guys threw rings at glass bottles in the hopes of winning stuffed animals for their girlfriends.

I walked straight to the Theta medieval castle, as tall as a two-story building. A line of people snaked out of the massive castle entrance: the mouth of a dragon, with four-foot-tall white teeth. Sun reflected off thousands of gold metal scales covering the dragon's body.

I saw a woman with a Theta shirt on standing at the entrance to the mouth. I pointed to my shirt with KAΘ on it, and she smiled and waved me past the line. I walked into the dimly lit mouth and stepped into the interior of the castle.

Rows of silver metal bleachers, enough to accommodate more than a hundred people, occupied the entire left half of the castle.

On my right sat a massive stage. Everything was painted to look like the inside of a medieval castle. Some Thetas were in costume, getting ready for the show. I saw several Thetas I recognized and sat with them to wait for the next show to start.

I couldn't believe that between all of us Thetas and our partner fraternity, Kappa Sigma, we had built this entire structure from scratch and outfitted it with electricity in just a few weeks. Our dues had covered the cost and we were donating all proceeds from the ticket sales to charity.

The medieval-themed musical started—much like one of the themed shows at Disneyland, with brightly colored costumes, singing, and dancing. Members of Theta and Kappa Sig had written and performed all the songs in the 45-minute musical. When it ended, massive cheers and a standing ovation erupted from the crowd.

At the end of the carnival we all walked over to a big stage. Thousands of students wearing sorority and fraternity letters packed the area. Someone walked to the front of the stage, picked up a microphone, and welcomed us to the Thurtene Carnival award ceremony.

We were competing against about six or seven other groups, other sororities and fraternities partnering together, all of whom had also built massive structures and performed original shows. Our group of Thetas and Kappa Sigs tensed up and watched the stage intently.

"The winners in the category of original themed musical are… Kappa Alpha Theta and Kappa Sigma!"

We all erupted in high fives and hugging. One of our group came back with the highly coveted Thurtene grand prize trophy and we cheered louder. Together, we all walked over to an after party at the

Kappa Sig fraternity house, holding the trophy high.

Frat boys welcomed us into their house by spraying champagne all over us. Music pumped loudly as the guys handed out beers and made mixed drinks. Between the beer and fuzzy navels, I got so drunk that night I had to go out to the side of the house and puke. Then I came back inside and danced some more.

At some point I made out with some senior Kappa Sig guy. The next weekend, he picked me up from my freshman dorm in his car and took me on a date to play miniature golf and eat at an Italian restaurant. He was squeaky clean and cute, but after the first date I never responded to his invitations for future dates. It was near the end of the school year and he was graduating.

Alone at the end of the year, I closed the door to my dorm room and turned off the light. I walked over to my boombox, popped in my Madonna *Immaculate Collection* CD, and cranked it up. I danced by myself underneath the glow in the dark stars I'd painted on the ceiling on my side of the room. The music enveloped me.

My freshman year was over. Most people had already left to go home, so the dorm was eerily quiet. I wasn't leaving until the next day.

When I finished dancing to my favorite song, "Rescue Me," I changed the CD to Nine Inch Nails. The pounding beats began, and I started to dance with abandon. After a while, I wore myself out and sat down, staring at my roommate's empty bed.

That night was the end of a tumultuous relationship with her. It had started with her alcohol poisoning and didn't get much better from there. I had spent many nights on the floor of other people's rooms to avoid her—and all the different guys she brought to our room. So many random guys on campus would awkwardly say "hi" to me and a slow recognition would come over me that it was just another one of Madison's hookups that I'd had to change clothes in front of because they were so inconsiderate—sitting there staring at me, not giving me any privacy.

When I'd asked Madison if she could just have guys sleep over on the weekend, so that I could get decent sleep before class the next day, her response was "No, this is my room too." This was also her response when I asked if, on the weekdays, she could turn the light off by midnight.

So now, a feeling of relief and excitement washed over me. I looked forward to having a different roommate sophomore year—a friend from my dorm! Excited, I popped in one of my Erasure CDs and got up and started to dance again. Thinking about Theta made me smile. For the first time, I felt (at least a little) popular. I had a feeling of belonging and a newfound confidence energized me.

I didn't know it yet, but this feeling of belonging wouldn't last long.

However, that last night in my freshman dorm, I felt excited for my flight the next day. I was headed to my summer job washing and folding guests' sheets and towels at Jackson Lake Lodge in Jackson Hole, Wyoming. I danced until I fell asleep.

PART TWO

SOPHOMORE YEAR

7

AN EX COMES OUT

September, Sophomore Year

Sitting on William's bed the first week of my sophomore year, I sensed that something was very wrong. He had asked me to come over to his dorm room to talk, but I couldn't imagine what about. *Does he want to get back together?*

I sat on one end of his neatly made bed, him on the other. Music played softly in the background as William fidgeted, looking everywhere but at me, his brow furrowed.

Finally, he blurted out, "I met someone over the summer." Before I had a chance to respond, he quickly added "A guy."

I remained silent for a moment. I felt my right hand clench reflexively, like I was going to punch through the mattress. William still didn't make eye contact and an uncomfortable silence ensued as he stared at the bed and said, "I'm bisexual."

As my body tensed and my fist clenched tighter, I blurted out the first thing that came to mind: "What are my sorority sisters going to think if they find out I dated someone bisexual?" This was probably one of the least supportive things I could have said, but I was in shock and unfortunately this was my gut reaction.

This was the early 1990s, before social media, before gay characters appeared in any mainstream media, and before celebrities were out —not even Ellen DeGeneres was out yet. I had never even heard of anyone being "out" as bisexual or gay, let alone met anyone openly LGBTQ before William. The only contact I'd had with LGBTQ people was hearing terms like "fagatron" and "lesbo" and "queer"—always in a derogatory context.

If I hadn't been so sheltered, I would have seen the signs. William wore Colors cologne by Benetton, always tucked in his button-down polos, and was clean-shaven, with minty Listerine breath. Clearly not the frat boy type, he was slightly effeminate. His love of Erasure, Madonna, and the Pet Shop Boys would have tipped me off if I'd known anything about gay culture. However, it did seem unusual that he never tried to convince me to have sex—a first, in my experience. But even so, the thought never occurred to me that William might not be straight.

Leaving William's room, I trudged back to my room. Quietly opening the door, I walked in, leaving the lights off. My roommate, Daniela, was nestled in bed sound asleep. I lay silently on my bed in the dark. The clock on my boom box read 2:30 a.m., but I was as wide awake as if I had consumed 10 shots of espresso. My head churned.

Something else was bothering me now—not just what my sorority sisters would think about me having dated someone bisexual. Restlessly I jerked my legs up, then down, then up, then down. I rolled to one side, then the other, then on my back, then my stomach, then back again. I couldn't relax. I couldn't get comfortable.

Thoughts of my past relationships poured through my

consciousness. I worried about where my thoughts were leading me. Something nagged at the corners of my mind—like the calm before a tornado, when an eerie stillness signals something isn't right, but you don't yet know what it is.

Prior to high school, I had kissed three boys. Zach, a generic, tall brown-haired guy was first. His crush on me began in sixth grade. We swam in his pool and played dominoes. The night of my first kiss, Zach and I whispered nervously in my bedroom in Dallas, the lights turned off. Zach said, "I'll write down what I want to do on a piece of paper and you do too. Then we'll read what the other one wrote."

We kneeled on the floor on opposite sides of my bed. I knew exactly what I wanted to write, but couldn't force my shaking hand to move. After several long minutes, Zach said, "You done?"

I softly said "No, not yet."

After several more minutes, I finally decided to write down what I really wanted to do. In cursive I wrote "I want to kiss you." I quickly folded the paper up and reluctantly threw it across the bed. He placed his in front of me. I snatched it and scampered into my walk-in closet to read it, shutting the door. Quickly I unfolded his paper—and it was blank!

What? He tricked me! How can I go back out there now that he knows I want to kiss him? I sat paralyzed in my closet, my face scorching hot.

After a few minutes I heard "You coming out?" right outside the door.

"I don't know."

"Come on."

I didn't know what to say and remained quiet for a moment.

Finally, he said, "I'm sorry I didn't write anything. I want to do the same thing you wrote."

Now I was utterly afraid to come out. My heart beat faster and my face became hotter. I didn't move. Slowly, the door handle started to turn and the door opened. Zach turned off the closet light and knelt in front of me. I sat cross-legged on the tan carpet and he leaned in and kissed me timidly.

All the sudden I heard "Kristin, where are you?" from the hallway. I jerked back and jumped up, turned on the closet light and rushed to turn on the light in my room, leaving Zach behind. I yelled back to my mom, "I'm in here," opening the door.

I broke up with Zach shortly thereafter. I can't remember any reason, in particular. I just decided to break up with him one day.

White Jeans Guy stole my second kiss while I was a seventh grader. I wore a pink satin dress and pearl-colored flats to the Valentine's dance at Westwood Junior High School. The dark gym glowed with colored lights. Red, pink, and white balloons bounced around in the vast space.

I danced with my few friends to the fast songs. Then the first slow song came on: "Crazy For You" by Madonna. Panic and excitement swept the gym. My friends and I hurried to the side, huddled together, hoping to be asked to dance. Chelsea whispered, "Look, there's a guy coming over here!"

An awkward boy tapped on Anna's shoulder and whispered something I couldn't hear, then turned and pointed across the gym. Anna nodded and the boy started walking away.

Chelsea jumped in, "What did he say?"

Anna looked at me and said, "His friend wants to dance with you!"

I said, "Me? Who is it?"

She pointed at a guy with white jeans, white tennis shoes, and a white button-down shirt. He had shoulder-length dark hair like a rock star. I didn't recognize him.

Anna then said, "He's a ninth grader!"

"What should I do?"

She squealed, "He's coming over here!"

He walked straight up to me and said, "D'ya wanna dance?"

I followed him to the center of the dance floor. He placed his hands on my waist and my arms circled his neck. I felt his thighs pressed against my legs. We turned around and around, not really going anywhere.

The song ended and I started to pull away. Another slow song began and he asked, "Wanna dance again?"

"Okay, but I've got to take off my shoes." I had blisters on my heels. I left my flats with my friends then rushed back.

This time he pulled me even closer. At the end of the song he asked, "Can I kiss you?"

He leaned down to kiss me. His tongue surprised me. We danced for a few more songs, until a fast song came on. Then I said, "I'm going to go dance with my friends."

When the lights in the gym came on, the four of us strolled to the exit. White Jeans Guy snuck up behind me, grabbed my arm, and said, "Can I have your phone number?" I tried to sound nonchalant, like this happened to me all the time, but inside I was thinking, *I can't believe a ninth grader wants my phone number!*

White Jeans Guy began to leave love notes and gifts on the front steps of my house. Then he started stopping by unannounced. I found out from one of my friends that he'd been suspended from school and I stopped returning his phone calls. Eventually his gifts stopped. We never kissed a second time.

In eighth grade, Vance captured my third kiss. He played the trombone but was cooler than a band geek; he looked like Barbie's Ken. In band, I sat on Vance's lap and we kissed a few times, but we never saw each other outside of school. He broke up with me the summer after eighth grade. Maybe because I was moving to Nashville? I never cried or remember feeling sad about it.

In the same middle school band as Vance and me, Brandi played the French horn. I played the trumpet. The summer after eighth grade, Brandi and I spent many days and nights together at Six Flags over Texas.

Every time she asked, "What do you want to ride?" I would respond "The Spinnaker!" a ride with swinging gondola cars that spun extremely fast until we were upside down. She would climb into the metal cage first and straddle the cushioned seat, leaning against the back. Then, I would squeeze into the cage and straddle the same seat, with my back against her chest. The door to our private cage would be closed by the attendant and it would slowly move forward, picking up speed until we whirled in a circle, warm wind on our skin.

Upside down, the cage pressed me hard against Brandi's chest behind me. Her breasts and body enveloped me. Her hot breath tickled my neck. I could smell her spicy yet sweet Obsession perfume. Adrenaline flooded my body, from my toes to the top of my head.

Though the intense high I felt from our rides on the Spinnaker was unmatched, I didn't attach any meaning to these feelings at the time. I just knew they were electrifying. I wanted the ride to never end. Four minutes was not enough. Seven rides were not enough. I wanted to be pressed up against her forever, breathing in the scent of her perfume.

One day, a downpour of rain started and we dashed from the roller coaster to the nearest overhang. As the rain poured down and the sky became blanketed in gray, people poured out of the park and it began to empty out.

"Do you want to stay?" she asked.

"Yes!"

Rain poured down, drenching our shorts and T-shirts as we laughed, running in the warm rain to the next ride. The air smelled earthy from fresh rain on the hot asphalt. There were no lines, so we rode my second favorite ride several times.

Dozens of racing cars that looked like Corvettes: brilliant reds, hot pinks, ocean blues filled an immense room. The cars were lined up in a circle on a racetrack that went up and down like rolling hills. I chose an empty green car with yellow stripes. I climbed in first and sat on the inside, and Brandi sat on the outside. An attendant closed our car door.

After a few moments, the lights turned off, briefly leaving us in darkness before bright multicolored lights enveloped us from all sides. The cars started to move slowly, beginning to undulate up and down on the track. As we started to pick up speed, white strobe lights flashed on and off, as "You Might Think" by the Cars blasted in the enclosed space. As we moved faster and faster, the force pulled me closer and closer to Brandi, until I was pressed against her shoulder. I held on to the metal bar in front of me, but I let it slip through my fingers, so I could feel her skin against mine. I relished the warmth of her arm, even though it was wet from the rain. The cool air-conditioning whizzed by our faces as we whirled around and around in circles, up and down on the track. The hairs on my arms stood up and I couldn't control my wide smile as our long hair whipped behind us, our bodies melding together. As the music began to slow, the pace of the cars decreased, and my smile started to fade, as I was no longer pulled toward her.

As we stopped, I slid away from Brandi and stepped out of the car. I looked at her and smiled. "Again? I bet there's no line!"

"Sounds great!"

We hustled outside, back into the rain, then back on the ride again. That day, we rode the Spinnaker and the Cars dozens of times. We stayed until after dark and the rides sparkled with lights. We ended our evening with the sweet richness of a warm funnel cake covered in powdered sugar, pulling pieces off, occasionally brushing fingers.

At the end of that summer, my family moved from Dallas to Nashville. Every night I listened to the radio in bed, waiting for Brandi's favorite song, "Broken Wings" by Mr. Mister, to come on. When the 80's ballad finally began playing, I imagined I was singing the words to Brandi while tears dripped down my face onto my pillow.

I spent night after night crying myself to sleep, thinking about Brandi and reliving those warm summer nights at Six Flags. I could still feel my body pressed against hers. I could still feel her breasts against me. I could still smell her Obsession perfume.

For months, I became consumed with how much I missed her and would cry and cry and cry, alone in my room. I replayed our rides on the Spinnaker, relishing both the intense pleasure of my thoughts as well as the intense pain of my longing.

Now, alone in my dorm room that night, I questioned my sexual orientation for the first time. Being straight was always a given— there was never another option. But now, remembering Brandi and our rides on the Spinnaker created an intense mixture of thrill, confusion, exhilaration, and fear. *Did my feelings mean anything? Did all women have feelings like these for other women? Do I want to be with a woman?* Until the night William told me he was bisexual, I had no conscious conflict about my sexual orientation. Now I could think of nothing else.

8

THANK YOU, *COSMO*

October, Sophomore Year

As I waited for William to arrive in my room, I wiped my sweaty palms on my jeans. I had asked him to come over, since I really needed to talk. My roommate, Daniela, was out.

My mind swirled as I sat on my bed, staring at the melting clock on Daniela's creepy Salvador Dali poster. Her unmade bed had a few engineering textbooks scattered on top.

All week I'd been questioning things I'd never questioned before. My brain was exploding with questions: question marks floating around my room, on the ceiling, in the air, in my closet, near the window. *What is my problem?*

Knock, knock. I was jolted from my internal dialogue. "Come in."

The door squeaked as it opened slowly and William popped his head around the corner. We hugged, and I sat on my bed and he sat on my desk chair. Daniela was at crew practice, so I knew we would be alone for at least another hour.

"So, what's up?" William asked.

"Oh, you know. The usual. Studying. Hanging out." I studied the permanent stains on the linoleum floor. "The semester just started and I already feel like I have tons of work."

"I know that's not what you wanted to talk about, right? What's really going on?"

I paused and fidgeted with my blanket. "You know, I've been thinking a lot about what you told me the other day. It's really been stressing me out." I continued to avoid eye contact.

"What do you mean? Why?" William had concern in his voice. "Are you still worried about your sorority and what they'll think?"

"Well, kind of. Not exactly. I mean, yes, but there's something else too."

"Okay…"

"I uh, just don't exactly know how to say this." I was twisting my blanket feverishly. I blurted out, "William, I'm freaked out that I might not be straight too." I held my breath.

Lightheartedly, he said, "Oh, don't worry. I'm sure you're just reacting to my news and it's nothing."

Is he right? Why do I even think I might not be straight? I'm such an idiot.

I said, "Are you sure? How can you know?"

"Well, only you would know for sure, but you're always hooking up with guys."

Hmm. Maybe he's right. Maybe I'm freaking out over nothing. "How do you know you like guys?"

"I think I've always known, at least on some level." He paused, looking deep in thought, then continued. "Maybe the opportunity just hadn't presented itself."

I paused, thinking, then asked, "I mean, but how did you know exactly?"

"Well, I've never had sex with a girl and never wanted to."

By this time William had told me he thought he was more gay than bisexual. *At least I know it wasn't just me.* "How is it different with guys?"

"Well, I've only been with one guy, but it was totally different."

"Like, different how?"

"Well, sex was great and I had orgasms. I wanted to have sex with him all the time."

Orgasm. I don't think anyone had ever used that word around me before. I had without question never said it out loud. Part of me wanted to change the subject, but another part wanted to know more. The uncomfortable silence between us was building. I needed to say something.

Words I couldn't quite control suddenly burst out of my mouth. "I have a confession to make." I felt my face burning, the heat creeping up from my neck. "I've never had an orgasm with a guy."

Looking a bit stunned, William said, "Really? But you've been with so many guys."

I took in a short breath. "Yeah, I have dated a lot of guys, but I never had an orgasm with any of them."

He looked perplexed. "Wow. I'm really surprised." He paused momentarily then continued, "Do you know why? Did they just not know what they were doing?"

I thought about my boyfriend James, during my senior year of high school. He came over the night before I was leaving for St. Louis to go to college. I had broken up with him during the school year, so we weren't together anymore, but he wanted to say goodbye and gave me two CDs, the Police's *Greatest Hits* and Madonna's

Immaculate Collection. I popped the Police into the new silver boom box my parents had bought me to bring to college.

We had never had oral sex before; in fact, I had never had oral sex at all. After making out for a while, he started going down on me, but I didn't feel much. I had a cold with a fever and didn't feel well and didn't know if it was because he wasn't doing it right, or I was sick, or the Nyquil messed with my libido, or the stress of leaving home for college the next day. It wasn't that exciting and I told him to stop after a few minutes.

"Maybe you're right. Maybe they didn't know what they were doing. I really have no idea."

William looked stumped. Looking at him, something else popped out of my mouth. "Okay, so I have something to say that's even more embarrassing. You promise not to tell anyone? I've never told anyone this before."

"Okay." He looked intrigued and leaned in.

I took in a deep breath and in a shaky voice said, "Uh, well, I've never actually had an orgasm before at all. I mean, not that I know of."

William's eyes widened. "Are you serious? What about when you masturbate? I mean, if you had you'd definitely know."

My heart pounded so loud I wondered if William could hear it. I wiped my sweaty palms on my jeans. I could feel the heat in my face spreading. "I've never masturbated," I said quickly.

Silence. Neither of us said a word. I couldn't look up.

He finally asked, "Why not?"

Continuing to talk to the floor, I said "Um, I don't know. It's never really occurred to me, I guess."

"Wow. That's just so surprising. I thought everyone did."

"Really? I wonder if girls are different. I guess I'm not even sure what to do. I don't know. We never talk about it." I shrugged.

He said, "Girls absolutely do it. They're always talking about masturbating and orgasms and sex in the *Cosmo* magazines I read."

"Really?"

William looked serious and concerned. "Yeah, I should give you a few to read. They're great—interesting articles."

The next time William stopped by, he brought some of his old *Cosmopolitan* magazines. I hid them and, when Daniela wasn't there, snuck them out like I was reading pornography. There were all sorts of articles about women fulfilling themselves sexually, the best sexual positions, and how most women don't achieve orgasm during traditional missionary position sex. There were articles talking about vibrators and masturbation and oral sex and how to please a man and how to ask for what you want in bed.

I was now dying to find out what it was like. I felt like an idiot that I was 19 years old and had never had an orgasm or even masturbated before. I wondered if I was the only girl in my sorority who was this clueless. I had never talked about the Big O with anyone other than William. The magazines even had tips on masturbating: using a vibrator and making the setting romantic with candles, bubble bath, dim lighting, and sexy music.

First of all, where in the world would I purchase a vibrator? It wasn't like they sold them in the campus bookstore. (This was before the Internet!) Two, there were no bathtubs in my dorm, so a bubble bath was out of the question. Three, I lived in a tiny room and had a roommate. I wasn't going to light candles and put on sexy music when Daniela left the room—what if she came back and saw me under the covers with candles and sexy music on?!?!

Despite the challenges, I was able to figure it out quickly. Thank you, *Cosmo*.

9

INSPIRED BY OBSESSION

October, Sophomore Year

"Here's your coffee," Daniela said with a big smile on her face. She handed me my large mug in the shape of a blue and silver Dallas Cowboys football helmet.

I sipped the steaming cup of Maxwell House International Café French Vanilla instant coffee with a touch of Kahlua. She turned off the hot pot. The sweet liquid burned my throat. Our empty Cup of Noodles still sat on our desks. I sipped from my mug as I tried to concentrate on my Physics textbook, rereading the same paragraph multiple times. My open notebook sat beside me on my desk. I hadn't written a single word.

We sat in silence as I attempted to read. Daniela sat on her comforter, which was covered with loud patterns of primary reds, blues, yellows, and greens. I could see her scribbling frantically in her notebook, then abruptly stopping. Then, she would look back at her book, pause, then start scribbling again. I saw her smile to herself several times as she worked, probably on an engineering problem set.

After we finished our coffee, brushed our teeth in the bathroom down the hall, and changed into sleep clothes, Daniela turned off the lights. I stared up at the glow-in-the-dark stars I had stuck on my side of the ceiling. The starry sky enveloped me. Normally this was calming, but I now dreaded this time of the day, because I could no longer escape my thoughts. Alone, with no distractions, I began again to replay past relationships in my mind. I didn't understand what my feelings meant and why I was so confused. Nothing was making sense.

After moving from Dallas to Nashville in time to start ninth grade, I bought imitation Obsession perfume from the drugstore. Brandi had worn the real version. In the morning before school, I held the cylindrical can that read "Inspired by Obsession," spraying the mist all over my body. I took a deep breath of the spicy sweetness and could almost feel Brandi next to me. As I walked between classes and smelled the faint scent of the perfume, warmth spread over my body as the smell brought me back to our days at Six Flags. During classes, I daydreamed about us in the Spinnaker, my body pressed against hers.

After class I changed into my burgundy and white volleyball uniform, the colors of my new high school, the University School of Nashville. On the way to our game, we packed into the team van like sardines. Wearing short shorts, my bare legs touched the legs of the two teammates I sat sandwiched between. Shoulder to shoulder, I could feel the warmth from their arms and legs. The blond hairs on my body stood at attention and my body tingled.

As I sat on the sidelines, I watched Emily, a tall senior girl, powerfully spike the volleyball over the net. She moved gracefully and commanded the court. As she scored a point, the other girls high-fived her.

On the drive home, I was lucky enough to sit next to Emily. I couldn't bring myself to talk to her. My hands were sweating from nerves and I couldn't think of anything but her leg touching mine. She chatted easily with the others, but I was petrified to speak.

When I turned 15, halfway through freshman year, I got a job bagging groceries at Kroger. I had been looking forward to getting a job for months and was finally old enough. When I first started, I rode my bike to work, but after several months I saved up enough for half the cost of a red Honda scooter; my parents agreed to pay for the other half. As I rode to Kroger in my red and white helmet my coworkers would yell, "Hey, Harley woman!" Although my scooter maxed out at 35 mph downhill with a tail wind, I felt cool.

I enjoyed evaluating a customer's groceries as they came down the conveyer belt and figuring out the best way to place them in the paper bags. I made sure the heavy items were on the bottom and fragile items were on top, making them fit neatly like pieces in a Tetris game. After placing the bags in the cart with care, I offered, "Can I take your groceries out to the car for you?"

As I followed customers to their cars, they usually asked me questions like "What do you want to do when you grow up?" I would answer, "I'm not sure. Maybe I'll be an architect. Or maybe a lawyer like my dad." If I were lucky, the housewife would tip me with a dollar bill. If I left my eight-hour shift with $5, I felt very accomplished.

The nights I worked late, I often saw a dark-haired guy come in at about 10 p.m., talk to a few of the more senior cashiers, then head to the back of the store. Sometimes when I started a shift at 7 a.m.

on the weekends, I saw him leave the store right after I got there.

One night when I worked late, I walked to the back of the store, pushing my cart of bathroom cleaning supplies, and saw him stocking the shelves with cereal boxes. As I passed him, he smiled at me. I could see the black Poison concert T-shirt underneath his white button down. The smell of cigarette smoke emanated from him.

Later that night, on my break, I bought my usual glazed doughnut in the grocery's dark and dingy "restaurant" and sat in a plastic booth.

The night stocker came in right after I sat down, bought a soda, and began walking toward me. "Hi, I'm Shaun. I see you around all the time. Can I sit with you?"

My heart sped up. My throat felt dry. "Sure."

That's where it all started. Every week when the next week's schedule was posted, I would rush to check it and see if my schedule overlapped with Shaun's. If I knew our schedules overlapped, I would try to bag groceries at his register or volunteer to clean the bathrooms so I could find him stocking groceries. I learned later that he had completed high school, but had no plans to attend college. His job as a night stocker was full-time and he lived in an apartment by himself.

For our first date, Shaun picked me up in a beat-up blue Pontiac Sunfire. Burger King wrappers covered the floor and the car smelled of cigarettes. Cassette tapes of Led Zeppelin and Whitesnake were scattered everywhere. We would drive to the park after work and hang out until five minutes before my curfew, and he would drive me home just in the nick of time. Sometimes we made out in his car for a few hours.

A few months into dating, he picked me up from work and we

drove straight to the parking lot next to the tennis courts where my dad and I often played. He turned off the ignition and rolled down my bucket seat for me, then rolled his down, and leaned in for a kiss. I loved the cigarette taste on his lips and the smell of it in his car and on his clothes. It felt dangerous and adult. He unbuttoned and took off the white button-down I had to wear to work. He took off his shirt too. We were now chest to chest, making out.

All the sudden, a hard knock on the window reverberated. We jumped. The windows had fogged up completely and we couldn't see out. A deep male voice said, "Roll down your window. This is the police."

I fumbled to find my shirt and cover myself. Shaun rolled down his window and cold air seeped in. The policeman looked inside the car and peered at me, shaking his head. "You can't park here. Get dressed and get out of the park."

Shaun was the bad boy and I was the good girl. He was dangerous and made me uneasy, in a good way. I liked to linger in front of school, so people could see him pick me up in his car.

Shaun once told me that "Sex isn't really all that it's cracked up to be. It's more trouble than it's worth." I had no idea what that meant. I had absolutely no interest in having sex. The closest we ever got was one night after we went to a haunted house. We parked exactly where the policeman had previously confronted us. After making out for an hour, Shaun stopped and said, "Don't you ever get bored of just kissing?"

I thought, *No, not really.* I'd seen the cartoon books that my parents kept in their bedroom drawer showing what sex is and how babies are made, and it didn't look all that fun.

I said, "Um, I'm not sure. I guess."

Just this one time, Shaun unzipped his pants and took my hand and slid it under his boxers. I drew my hand back quickly. After five months this was the furthest I let things go. During my sophomore year in high school, our relationship fizzled. We saw less and less of each other over time. I never cried about it. I just kept busy with school and work.

Now, staring up at my dorm ceiling, something nagged at the back of my mind. I couldn't put my finger on it. A feeling deep inside me told me something wasn't right. I was questioning everything about my dating life and my relationships, searching for some meaning, some sign that everything was normal. That I was normal.

10

GET OFF ME

November, Sophomore Year

When Ted and I entered the dance hall with Daniela and her date, it was already filled with dozens of my sorority sisters and their dates—all guys, of course. Daniela had just joined Theta, which I was very excited about. For our yearly semi-formal dance, all my sisters were wearing dresses. Ted blended in with all the guys in khaki pants and a light blue button-down, but I wore black jeans and a white button-down. Nobody said anything about my casual outfit (to my face, that is). I couldn't bring myself to wear my one dress or my one skirt yet again.

Ted and I had met a few weeks before in our dorm. He asked me out on a date when we first met, which was unusual; the college culture was mostly people just hooking up on campus, rarely going out for formal dates off-campus. I thought it was sweet. He was Asian, about five-foot-eight, and very buff, but lean; his short hair was neat, parted on the side.

On our first date, he was wearing nicely fitted jeans and a polo shirt. A few blocks from campus, we entered what looked like a small church from the outside. Inside was a casual Italian restaurant that was known for its pizza. Stained-glass windows covered the high ceilings.

Since that date, we had hung out a few times, including going to the gym together. He focused on lifting weights and I split my time between weights, the step machine, and sit-ups.

At the semi-formal, I saw a few sisters that I was close to and we joined them on the dance floor. The loud music made it difficult to talk, so we all danced on the hardwood floor in the semi-darkness, surrounded by black and gold balloons and streamers. The tables were scattered with people drinking and snacking.

After dancing to the pumping music with Ted, my sisters, and their dates for a couple of hours, Ted and I walked back to my dorm room. My roommate was staying elsewhere, but just in case I left a red sock tied around the doorknob. This was our signal for "Stay away, I'm hooking up right now."

Ted tried to take my hand and kiss me, but I pulled away reflexively. I went over and flicked the light switch off. Light still came through the window from the streetlights outside. I put on a Depeche Mode CD and sat on the bed. He tried to kiss me again, and again, I turned away. He seemed a little confused.

He took off his button-down, exposing his smooth, almost hairless skin and his well-defined shoulders, strong pecs, and six-pack—all his time in the gym had paid off. He reached around and unhooked my bra, then took all his clothes off.

Things progressed, but I continued to turn away if he tried to kiss me on the lips. At some point, he got on top of me, thrusted slowly, and looked at me, asking, "Does this feel good, baby?"

Not only does it not feel good, but frankly it's quite boring. I didn't say anything.

He moaned again and says, "Feels good, right?"

I couldn't help myself and said, "No, not really."

He stopped abruptly and looked at me. I looked at him and said, "Get off me."

He didn't move. He continued to hold himself above me, though he'd stopped thrusting.

I repeated, "Get off me" and he removed himself slowly.

"Did I do something wrong?"

I covered my body with my hands and said, "Just leave."

He continued to stare at me as he got up, a confused look on his face. I turned away from him and got dressed, then just sat on the bed waiting for him to leave.

After he closed the door behind him, I sat on my bed listening to the haunting music of Depeche Mode, a few tears dripping down my cheeks. I wasn't sure exactly why I was crying. Things just didn't feel right. I lay back, staring at the stars on the ceiling and listening to the music on repeat until I fell asleep.

A few days later, Daniela and I had just gotten back from dinner at the Bear's Den and were laughing about something when we heard a knock on the door. We turned to look and Ted was peering around the door, which was ajar. I had successfully avoided him for the past couple of days.

"Can we talk?" he asked.

Daniela and I just looked at each other. I had told her everything about Ted. She gave me an understanding look.

I sighed and said, "Okay, sure."

He smiled and said, "You want to go to my room?" I followed a few steps behind him and we took the elevator a few floors up, to his single room. His textbooks were meticulously arranged on his desk and bookshelves. On one of our earlier dates, he'd told me he wanted to be an actuary after graduating. I had quickly changed the subject; anything would have been more interesting.

He sat on his bed, and I sat on the opposite side. He looked down at his lap and said, "I really like you."

I didn't know what to say, so I sat there while an uncomfortable pause passed between us.

He continued, "I'd really like to still go out with you."

I could have counted the number of times we had hung out on two hands. We had met just a little over a month before and it felt very casual to me. We had never had sex before semi-formal and it didn't really count, since it was cut short.

I said, "I'm sorry. I'm just not interested."

He put his head in his hands and started crying. I didn't say anything while he quietly cried. He stopped after a few minutes and pulled his hands away from his face, wiping his hands on his jeans.

I said, "I'm sorry, Ted."

He caught his breath, looked up and said, "Did I do something wrong?"

I hesitated for a moment, thinking. "It's nothing specific. I just don't want anything right now. I'm really sorry."

He peered at me while blinking his sad puppy dog eyes. "Can you just give me one more chance? One more date?"

"Ted, no. I'm sorry."

His shoulders slumped. I could tell he was fighting back tears.

"Okay."

I got up and leaned in and gave him a hug. He hugged back tightly. His grasp lingered. When he finally let go, I looked at his sad eyes again, then left his room while he sat motionless on his bed. I felt strangely unsettled, but didn't know why. As I walked back to my room, I tried to (unsuccessfully) shake it off.

11

ABNORMAL PSYCHOLOGY

January, Sophomore Year

I'd had Alex's phone number for more than two weeks and thought about calling her every day. I knew she was expecting to hear from me, because William had told her I would call. He'd met Alex when he attended a GLBA (Gay, Lesbian, Bisexual Alliance) meeting on campus—Alex was the club's president.

I was about to talk to a real-life lesbian for the first time and was terrified. My lungs burned and it was hard to catch my breath. The phone shook as I held it in my hand. I clenched the phone and dialed, but halfway through her number I hung up.

I paced around my dorm room, wondering what she would be like. I pictured a deep, confident, no-nonsense voice answering. After taking a few breaths to try to calm myself, I picked up the phone again. This time I got through the entire number. It felt like forever before the ringing began. I was afraid if it took too long for her to pick up, I would lose my nerve.

Ring...ring...ring. She picked up. "Hello." Her warm, clear voice caught me off guard.

I froze. *Should I hang up?* I still could. My breathing felt labored.

"Um, hi, this is Kristin. I'm a friend of William's. He gave me your number." I stopped abruptly. A pause lingered.

"Hey! William told me you might call."

I felt out of breath and couldn't immediately speak. After what felt like a very long pause, I said, "Yes, well…um, I was calling because I just, I'm just a little confused about…. Well, I'm not sure if I'm straight."

This was the second person I had ever said this to, William being the first.

I quickly continued, "And, um, well, William just thought you might be a good person to talk to. I'm just not really sure what to do." I stopped and waited, clenching the phone.

In an upbeat voice, Alex said, "Sure. I'd be happy to talk. It would be good to meet in person."

At the thought of meeting her in person, I felt out of breath again. I tried to take another deep breath, so I could respond. "Um, sure, okay."

Alex responded, "I know we're in the same Abnormal Psychology class. Do you want to meet after class on Thursday? We could go to the student union and talk."

I didn't know we were in the same class. I wondered how she knew. The words "Um, yeah" stumbled out of my mouth.

For the next two days, I had a hard time concentrating on my reading at the library. I couldn't help imagining what Alex would be like. I pictured her with a crew cut, combat boots, a black leather biker jacket, white tank top, and rugged men's jeans. I imagined her tough, with a manly walk. Fear coursed through my body as I imagined meeting her. I thought about cancelling, but an unknown force propelled me toward the encounter.

On Thursday, the day we were set to meet, I felt like I had drunk five shots of espresso. I entered the lecture hall right before class started at 2:30 p.m. About 400 students packed the hall, chatting, squeezing into their seats, and taking out their notebooks. I looked for my sorority sisters in the crowd and squeezed into a seat they'd saved for me; KAΘ, KΣ, Σχ, ZBT, and ΣAE plastered on baseball caps, T-shirts, and sweatshirts surrounded me on all sides. I knew all these letters and what fraternity or sorority they referred to, since I was required to memorize the Greek alphabet as part of my sorority initiation.

I had made sure not to wear my letters that day, which was not as easy as it sounds. Shirts with letters were a wardrobe staple of every Greek on campus. Every event was commemorated with a Theta shirt; a store off-campus existed whose sole purpose was to provide hundreds of choices of colors and patterns of letters. I wore my letters all the time, but on this day I'd aimed for anonymity.

Usually in class, I listened intently to the professor and took copious notes. Today, I fidgeted in my chair and chewed on the plastic cap of my pen. I alternated between staring absentmindedly at the professor and stealing glances to the right side of the lecture hall, where Alex had said she would be sitting. She said she had blond hair and would be sitting next to her roommate, who was tall with brown hair. On the phone, she had said she already knew who I was, so would be able to find me. I tried to keep my glances quick, so my sisters didn't catch me staring. I couldn't find Alex anywhere.

The class dragged on. I wasn't absorbing anything the professor said, even though it was my favorite class. I was fascinated to learn about mental illness, as I'd had some exposure to it in my family.

My mom's only sister had chased her around the house with a knife during her teens and ended up institutionalized for her entire adult life, with a diagnosis of schizophrenia. My sister had major depression and drug addiction, which probably led to her suicide attempt. My dad was hospitalized during law school at Vanderbilt with what he said was an anxiety disorder; he had become paralyzed from the waist down, although there was no physiological reason for it. Eventually the paralysis vanished and he was able to leave the hospital. It took a long time before he fully recovered from the anxiety.

In Abnormal Psychology I had learned that homosexuality had up until recently been classified as a mental disorder in the DSM-II— the Diagnostic and Statistical Manual of Mental Disorders, a catalog of all mental illness diagnoses and the guiding principles of our class. In the DSM-III-R in 1987, the version in use when I took Abnormal Psychology, the category of "ego-dystonic homosexuality" had finally been eliminated, but many psychologists used the category of "sexual disorders not otherwise specified" to continue to include homosexuality as a mental disorder.

Trying to be stealthy, I continued to look around for Alex. I didn't see any angry-looking tough girls with short blond hair. I started wondering how we would meet up without my sisters noticing. *What if they can tell she's gay and think I am too because I know her?* I didn't want my sorority sisters to see me with her. I remembered back to the last sorority rush, when one of my sisters had said about a rushee, "She looks like a lesbo. We don't want anyone like that in our sorority. I'm not voting for her." My other sisters just nodded and didn't say anything to contradict her. That moment was burned into my brain.

Maybe I should go out the left side and escape my friends, then

*go to the bathroom, then when they're all gone, I can meet Alex
and nobody will know.*

As I was mulling over my options, I heard the professor ending
class and was jolted out of my thoughts. Everyone was already
shuffling out of the aisles. I quickly stuffed my notebook and pen
in my backpack.

My heart started racing as I tried to quickly decide what to do. I
stood there in the middle of the row, then started to move left, away
from where Alex was sitting. I moved with the crowd toward the
back of the hall, making sure not to look around, as I really didn't
want Alex to approach me now. I needed to be clear of all my sisters
first. As I reached the exit, I hung back and let my sisters get ahead
of me, hoping they would keep moving until they were out of sight.
I ducked over to the side of the hall in the stairwell and looked out
as the crowd began to dwindle.

Now I began to worry that maybe Alex had forgotten. My heart
fell at the thought. I crept out of the stairwell and looked around,
not seeing anyone I thought could be her. Then I peered back into
the lecture hall. The professor was packing up his belongings and
a few students waited to talk to him. I turned around and exited
the building, looking all around. I half expected Alex to have come
to class on a Harley, but I only saw a few bikes locked up outside.

Suddenly, I heard, "Kristin. Hey, it's Alex!"

Her pretty face, petite body, and blond bob were not what I was
expecting. In fact, she didn't look like a lesbian at all, or at least
what I thought a lesbian looked like. She wore jeans and a sweatshirt
like just about every other student on campus.

"Hey," I said quietly, my eyes darting around to make sure none of
my sorority sisters were nearby. Luckily, I didn't see anyone I knew.

She smiled at me, sending shivers down my arms even though it was sunny out. "You cool with going over to the student union?" she said with confidence.

"Yeah, that sounds good," I mumbled, looking at my feet.

There was silence between us as we started to walk the five minutes across campus to the Rat. On the way I spied a few people I knew and hoped they didn't see me. We walked into the student union and down the stairs to the basement.

The underground part of the student union was mainly known for the bands that played on Thursday nights. We entered the large, dimly lit room, with a few booths on the perimeter and a hardwood stage at the far end. As we slid into the booth, its vinyl peeling away with age, the stale smell of the air felt confining.

Alex dove right in. "So tell me, what makes you think you might not be straight?"

I checked to see if I knew any of the dozen or so people scattered around the large space, then leaned in and started to talk in a hushed tone.

"Um, well, when William came out to me I started to think about how I really felt about guys and girls. I couldn't help but replay a bunch of my past relationships with guys. And, I think I might have had a crush on a girl in junior high school, but I'm not sure. I'd never met anyone gay before, so I'd never really thought about it. Then I started to get confused."

I stopped and looked up at Alex. She was listening intently and nodding, but didn't say anything.

I stared at my hands and started again. "I've dated a lot of guys and they're okay. But now I'm beginning to wonder if I have feelings for girls too. I don't know what they mean. I've never been with a girl. I just don't know. And I just don't know how you know. I just can't stop thinking about it and I don't know what to do."

I stopped and slowly looked up at her.

She nodded again, like she understood what I was saying. She asked, "Have you had sex with guys?"

I fidgeted in my seat and took a deep breath. "I've had sex with one guy, just a few times. And one other guy once, kind of." I couldn't believe I was telling this to someone I didn't even know.

"Did you like it?"

I glanced around me again. "It's okay I guess. I told Jake—the guy I was dating kind of, off and on—that I don't really want to have sex but that I'm okay with oral sex and using hands. He said he's fine with that, so that's what we would typically do when we hooked up."

Alex leaned in toward me. "Do you want to be with girls?"

I could feel my shoulders tense up. I stared at my lap.

I lowered my voice and said, "I don't really know. Maybe. I mean, I never really thought about it until William came out to me. Now I feel like I notice things I didn't notice before. Maybe I've been attracted to girls before, but nothing ever happened. Now I think about what it might be like."

"What kinds of things do you notice that you didn't notice before?"

"Well, like when this one girl from my sorority sits really close, or when she takes my hand at a party, trying to get through the crowd."

"How does that make you feel?"

I paused and tried to think about it. I said, "Sometimes excited and a little scared." I could feel myself blush and I started to get self-conscious. "I'm scared of what it might mean. I mean, does that mean anything?"

Alex paused and thought for a minute. "Maybe you could be bisexual."

Still clenching my hands, I said, "I don't know. Maybe." I paused, then looked up at her. She was at full attention. "What should I do?"

She quickly said, "Have you ever read *Curve,* or *Out,* or *On Our Backs*?"

"No. What are those?"

"They're gay magazines. You can buy them at a gay and lesbian bookstore."

Gay and lesbian bookstore?! I had no idea such a thing existed, and I couldn't imagine being able to walk into one. This was before you could order magazines or books on the Internet, so I would have no choice but to physically walk in. Despite my fears of being seen in a gay bookstore, I would soon get my hands on a magazine.

12

SMEAR THE QUEER

February, Sophomore Year

Cacti and wild bluebonnets filled my parents' backyard: the same Austin three-bedroom single-story brick house I had lived in before I left for college. A southwestern theme with earthy tones infused the interior.

I had grown up in Dallas from kindergarten through eighth grade. My dad worked as a lawyer at American Airlines, negotiating airline contracts all over the world. He traveled frequently, and often worked late; my sister and I mostly saw him on weekends. My mom worked at the Environmental Studies Center, giving tours to school kids and occasionally substitute-teaching. Every Sunday morning, instead of going to church or synagogue like everyone else who lived in Dallas, our tradition was to go out to breakfast. The four of us would take turns choosing the diner—IHOP, Denny's, or Jim's.

Sunday afternoons, my dad and I would watch the Dallas Cowboys game together—Roger Staubach and Danny White were the reigning quarterbacks. During halftime, my dad and I would throw the Nerf football in the front yard.

By about 6 p.m., my mom would be working hard in the kitchen. The smell of artichoke cooking and the lemon butter of the hollandaise sauce enticed our senses. Next came the scent of baked potatoes in the oven.

After the game, my dad would get the top sirloin out of the fridge and add a liberal amount of garlic salt and pepper, then throw it onto the indoor grill next to the stove. The eight-track played Placido Domingo, Dolly Parton, or Earl Scruggs. The four of us would pile butter, sour cream, chives, and imitation bacon bits on our potatoes, then dig in.

After dinner, my dad would ask "Who wants to go to Baskin Robbins?" with a big grin on his face. He had just as much of a sweet tooth as my sister and me. Marsha and I would scream "Us!" and scamper to the Chrysler minivan.

When I called to check in with my parents the middle of sophomore year, and they asked how things were going, the voice in my head screamed, *I feel like I'm going insane! I might not be straight and I'm freaking out! I'm having a hard time focusing and my grades are worse than they've ever been. I feel so isolated, like I have nobody to talk to. I feel so alone.*

Instead I said, "Not much. Just the usual classes."

"What are you taking this semester?" my mom asked.

"I'm taking Statistics, Abnormal Psychology, Introduction to Women's Studies, and Fiction Writing." I hoped she wouldn't notice that I'd only listed four classes—I was also taking Psychology of Homosexuality.

"That sounds interesting. Which class do you like best?"

My favorite class was Psychology of Homosexuality, but I was not going to say that. My head felt like a volcano about to erupt.

Impulsively I blurted "There's something that's really been bothering me lately."

"What's wrong?"

Like lava out of a volcano, I spewed, "I'm not sure if I'm straight. I don't know, but I think I could be bisexual or maybe gay."

All was quiet. I tried to catch my breath as I waited for her response.

I had one thing to my advantage in this situation. My parents were not religious, despite both being raised in Nashville in Christian families. My mom's parents forced her to attend church on Sundays and she hated the bigotry she saw in the church. She saw her parents and people in the church use religion and the Bible to justify their racism and condemnation of anyone who was not exactly like themselves. She wanted to escape the conservatism of her upbringing—and was then told that women were not permitted to major in geology at Vanderbilt, where she attended college. The university justified it by saying it wasn't appropriate for women to join men in the required fieldwork. My mom majored in biology instead.

When my parents met, she knew my dad was the one. He had shed his own conservative upbringing by attending the University of Chicago, an extremely liberal school. My dad had an African-American roommate for three years, which was unheard of in the 1950s. My dad thought religion was something that caused wars and that God was a myth; he was an atheist. So, at least I didn't have to worry about my parents believing that I would go to Hell if I were gay.

I could hear my mom breathing into the receiver. She took some time before responding. "Well, don't do anything you'll regret. You haven't, have you?"

Her response knocked the wind out of me.

"Um, no. I haven't done anything yet."

She responded in a matter of fact tone, "You need to be careful. You could get AIDS."

It was 1993 and there was a lot of talk of AIDS. I had never met anyone with AIDS, but I knew people were dying from it everywhere. A headache started to pulse in my right temple. Now I was worried about something new. Little did I know at the time, I was far less likely to contract the virus as a lesbian than I would have as a straight person!

She continued in a strong voice, "I just don't want you to do anything you'll regret. Your life will be very hard if you are gay. Just don't do anything without really thinking about it."

This was not making me feel better. Anxiety rattled my bones.

She abruptly said, "Your dad wants to talk to you. I'll let you talk to him."

My dad got on the phone and said in his commanding lawyer's voice, "I agree with your mother. Don't do anything you'll regret."

What does that mean exactly?

He then proceeded, "You know, when I was in college, I knew someone gay and I briefly wondered if that would ever be something I'd want for myself."

What? I thought to myself. *Huh?*

Continuing, he said, "But, in the end it didn't matter. I knew I wanted marriage and a family and that can't happen if you're gay. I knew I didn't want to have to hide. It was an easy choice. It really wasn't a choice at all."

I hadn't even thought about that. I had never really fantasized about getting married or having kids—but what if I wanted to down the line? *This is even worse than I thought.*

He said, "We just worry about you. Being gay is hard and we just want you to really think about it before you do anything."

When I hung up my head pounded with the new worries cascading in. Suddenly, thoughts of playing "Smear the Queer" in elementary school in Dallas hurtled though my brain. A boy from the neighborhood would throw a Nerf football as high as he could, straight up in the air. Then, all of us would try to jump up and catch it, jostling each other in the process. Whoever caught the Nerf football was anointed the "Queer" and had to then run around the yard, sprinting for their life. Everyone else would try to tackle him (or her if it was me), slamming him to the ground. Then the whole process would start all over again. It now dawned on me that I didn't know exactly what a queer was at the time, but knew enough to know it was the worst possible thing you could be, worthy of being "smeared." Now I knew what they meant.

Will I get AIDS if I'm gay? Will I be able to get married or have kids? Will my life be harder? Will I lose all my friends? Will Daniela and my other sorority sisters reject me or kick me out? As I sat with the phone still on my lap, I started to cry. Before long I was sobbing uncontrollably.

13

THE PSYCHOLOGY OF HOMOSEXUALITY

March, Sophomore Year

The semester before, William had told me he was signing up for a spring class called "The Psychology of Homosexuality: Social and Psychological Aspects." The class description listed topics such as internalized homophobia, the coming out process, religion and homosexuality, parents' reactions, laws that affect gay people like sodomy, discrimination, and marriage, and the history of the gay community.

"You should take it too!" he said.

"Ha ha, yeah," I said. I continued, talking quickly as my thoughts spewed out. "Aren't you worried that your parents will see it and ask you about it? Or what if you apply to graduate schools, and they see it and know you're gay? What if you're trying to apply for a job and they see it on your transcript?" I stopped, out of breath.

William's brow furrowed. "Hmm, I don't know. My parents have never asked to see my transcript. I don't know about the rest—I guess that stuff could happen. I just really want to take the class."

"It does sound really interesting."

Over the next couple of days, I thought a lot about it. *I am a psych major, so maybe I can pass it off as just part of the requirements. But what if people think I'm gay because I'm in the class? I guess I could just say it's for my major and is the only class that fits my schedule.*

One day toward the end of the semester, I sat for a long time in my dorm room with a scantron sign-up form in my hands. All I needed to do was to bubble in the circles next to the five classes I wanted to take. I had already filled out four of the five bubbles. I held my #2 pencil in my hand and chewed on it, tasting the wood in my mouth. Yellow paint flakes stuck on my lips, and I tried to wipe them off, then moved up the pencil to an area I hadn't yet chewed on.

I took the pencil out of my mouth and held it poised over the form. Something was compelling my hand to mark the bubble next to "Psychology of Homosexuality." I tried to hold back, but it felt like some invisible force kept pulling it back to that space. My rational mind said, *Don't do it! This is what your parents are talking about. Don't do something you'll regret. All sorts of unknown bad things could happen if you take this class!* I could hear my mom's voice in my head.

I quickly filled in the bubble for "The Psychology of Homosexuality," placed the form in a folder, and stuffed the folder in my backpack.

The next day, thoughts raced through my head as I walked to the psychology building to meet with my adviser. The wind whipped through my hair and I shivered, pulling my coat tighter as I walked past the barren trees and dead grass. *What will he say when I show him my classes? Will he think I'm gay?*

When I got there, there were a few students sitting on the floor outside his doorway, waiting. I sat on the floor with my back against the wall, behind the last student. I took my scantron form out of my backpack and turned it over, so nobody could see it.

His door opened, a student exited, and the next student went in. I jiggled my knee up and down, until the person next to me gave me a dirty look. Then I started chewing on my fingernails.

Eventually it was my turn. The door opened and the student before me walked out. I poked my head in the doorway and my adviser said, "Kristin, come on in." I sat on the wooden chair across from his desk, which was covered in student papers and books. He asked to see my schedule.

I handed it over and he began to scan it. I started chewing my fingernails again. He read out loud, "Psychological Statistics. Good. Psychology of Homosexuality?" He looked up at me. "What prompted you to want to sign up for that class?" I couldn't tell if he was just curious or disapproving.

I continued to chew on my fingernails. Then I looked down and said, "It fits my schedule. It's at a good time." I held my breath.

He continued to look at me. Then he quickly glanced at his watch and said, "Okay. It does help fulfill your psych requirements. That's fine."

Sitting next to William in class, I noticed Alex sitting nearby. I whispered, "William, you didn't tell me Alex was in here!"

"Oh, yeah. She is. Do you want to sit by her?" he asked with a smirk.

"No, I mean…well, sure, maybe next class." I felt my face reddening.

The next class, when I saw William, he was sitting next to Alex. I stopped in my tracks. I hadn't seen or talked to her since we met after Abnormal Psychology class. A couple of other students said "excuse me" and I moved to the side to let them pass. William and Alex were laughing about something. I took a deep breath and walked toward them, their backs to me as they sat facing the front of the room.

As I got to them, I said, "Hey, guys."

Simultaneously they both said "Hey!"

Someone was sitting on the other side of William, so I sat by Alex. She said, "So, how are things?"

I fumbled with my backpack, trying to get my notebook and pencil out. She continued, "I mean, after we talked."

I shifted in my seat. I absolutely did not want to talk about this in public. "Um, I don't know. About the same."

Luckily, I was saved by the professor, who started class right in the nick of time.

Sitting so close to Alex, my nerve endings felt raw. I felt feverish and chilly at the same time. I was hyperaware every time she moved a muscle, wrote something, or looked away from the professor. I could feel the warmth of her shoulder near mine. When she wrote something on a piece of paper, tore it off, and passed it over to me, I felt a wave of electricity. The note said, "How many people in here do you think are gay?"

About 150 students sat scattered throughout the medium-size lecture hall, sitting in old wooden seats with folding wooden desks that swiveled. I looked around at the students. *Hmm.* Nobody really looked gay to me—though I wasn't sure how you could tell. *Well, I know Alex and William are, so that's two.* I wrote "5" and passed it back to her.

Alex looked at the paper then over to me, smiling. She wrote something else on the piece of paper, folded it, and slid it back, brushing my arm lightly with hers. Tingling spread all over my body, down to my feet. I felt paralyzed.

After a moment, I was able to focus enough to read what she wrote. "No way. 75 people. I bet half the people in here are gay or at least will have figured it out by the end of college."

How can that possibly be? I looked over at her and mouthed "Really?" She nodded back.

I looked around again at the students in the class. William and Alex were still the only gay people I knew at this point. I didn't know if she was right, but it felt good and a little scary to think there were so many.

The entire semester, William, Alex, and I sat next to each other on the right side of the room toward the back—by far my favorite three hours each week. I looked forward to it all week and tried my best to sit next to Alex. We passed notes and the accidental (or were they?) touches seemed to get more frequent and bolder. She often touched my shoulder or my hand when leaning in to tell me something. She'd whisper something in my ear, and I could feel her lips touch my hair, her warm breath on my neck. My senses felt alive, the closeness with Alex dizzying. Between classes I fantasized about her and replayed every moment of my time with her.

I also learned some seriously disturbing facts about homosexuality. I learned that gay people couldn't legally get married. I learned that sodomy laws in many states were designed as a way to put gay people in jail, enforced only against gay people. Many people got fired for being gay, couldn't get housing, or couldn't adopt children—and it was *legal* to discriminate in this way. Many kids got kicked out of the house after coming out to their parents, and gay teen suicide attempts were four times that of heterosexual youth. Also, gay bashing was common and usually not punished by law.

My emotions during class overwhelmed me, flipping me between fear, excitement, anxiety, interest, and sadness. I longed for each class, despite what I was learning about the depressing reality of being gay.

14

FOUR GUYS IN ONE NIGHT

May, Sophomore Year

The smell of stale Budweiser, cheering frat boys, and champagne spraying through the air welcomed us. My 100+ sorority sisters and I began to file into the fraternity house at about 10 p.m. Music pounded in the dimly lit house. Daniela and I had each already consumed two shots of Bacardi before the party.

Frat boys ushered us into the "bar area." I heard people in front of us ordering "mind eraser," "fuzzy navel," and "screwdriver."

When we got to the front of the line a beefy guy asked us, "Whaddya want to drink?"

The saying, "Beer before liquor, never sicker. Liquor before beer, never fear" had been imprinted into my brain in college. So, I responded, "Coke and JD."

We got our drinks and drank them while vibrating to Def Leppard's "Pour Some Sugar on Me." Almost two hundred frat boys and sorority girls began the process of getting wasted and searching for a potential hookup. After grabbing another coke and

JD for myself, I was just beginning to feel a strong buzz.

Hot bodies crowded on the hardwood dance floor. No doubt the frats had learned that carpet was no match for such a large quantity of spilled beer, cigarette ashes, and greasy pizza. It was probably against the law to have that many people packed in such a small space. As I gyrated to "Push It" by Salt-N-Pepa, a generic All-American frat guy started dancing with me. Quickly his hands circled my waist and our bodies pressed closely together. He kissed me with a wet tongue of beer.

After a few sloppy seconds I pulled away and said, "I'm getting another drink." I grabbed Daniela.

"Who was that guy you were kissing?"

"I have no idea!" I yelled over the loud music.

After two hours of dancing, a few beers, and a make-out session with a different random guy, I was feeling a bit hazy from the alcohol. A third generic frat guy began dancing with me. As we started to make out, I felt someone's hand grip mine and drag me toward the door. Rachel, our sober sister for the night, said, "We need to talk" with a scowl on her face. She forcefully dragged me into the chilly night. Rachel said the president of our sorority had asked her to retrieve me because of my uncharacteristically erratic behavior.

Rachel led me down fraternity row toward the tennis courts. Wash U had 11 fraternities, with seven frat houses in a row on campus and four other houses off campus. There were seven sororities on campus too, but no sorority houses, only small suites in the Women's Building. I had heard that in St. Louis more than three unrelated women living in the same house together was considered a brothel and thus illegal—which was why we didn't have sorority houses.

I think this rumor was actually true.

Rachel and I sat alone behind the tennis courts, away from the noise and action on frat row.

"Are you okay?" she asked. "It's not like you to go kissing all those random guys."

No, I'm not okay at all. Something is wrong with me.

I stared into the night, across the intramural soccer fields to the buildings that housed classrooms. Small groups of students stumbled toward the dorms from the frat houses, talking animatedly. It was past 1 a.m.

I wanted to tell Rachel what was on my mind, but the words stuck in my throat. I was terrified of her reaction and of my sorority's reaction if they found out I might not be straight. I thought about all the good times I'd had with my new sisters over the past year and a half. I scored goals on the Theta intramural soccer team, spent late nights studying in the library with sisters, chatted over lunch in the sorority suite, spent every Sunday night in chapter meetings, volunteered at charity events, won the Thurtene Carnival grand prize trophy, and danced the night away at many Theta parties. Several of us Thetas drove to Washington, D.C. to march in a pro-choice rally, chanting and holding KEEP ABORTION LEGAL signs. Three sisters in my pledge class and I spent spring break in Florida, partying at dance clubs, laughing late at night, and sprinting to all the rides at Disney World. At the thought of losing all of this, I was petrified.

I silently stared at my black topsiders for what felt like hours. The tennis courts slowly spun around me. My head throbbed and my hands shook. I felt conflicted. Keeping my secret in made me feel so alone, but the risk of being the only out sorority girl on campus felt like bungee jumping with an old frayed cord that could snap at any moment.

I couldn't look at Rachel. I shivered in the cold.

"Are you okay?" she repeated.

On the verge of tears, I continued to stare at the ground and gripped the frigid concrete we were sitting on. Still looking down, I took a deep breath and blurted out, "I think I might be gay."

Silence.

More silence, as the cold air chilled me.

Even more silence. I shivered again.

Rachel curtly hugged me and said, "It's going to be okay. Let me get you home."

The hug felt awkward. Although she didn't say anything overtly negative, it was what she didn't say that left me feeling insecure. She didn't express empathy about how hard the situation must be, ask me more questions to understand how I was really doing, or say how glad she was that I felt comfortable confiding in her. It felt like an obligatory hug, then avoidance.

She walked me slowly and silently back to my dorm room. I stuffed my hands in my pockets and swerved a bit as we walked. I didn't dare look at Rachel. Despite what she said, I didn't really feel accepted or supported. Her distant body language and tone told me a different story. She left me at the front entrance to my dorm. "Get some sleep and drink water."

The drinks I had consumed earlier had erased my inhibitions enough to speak my secret aloud. This really is the one major benefit of alcohol. It certainly wasn't the puking, spinning rooms, or next-day regrets that attracted me to it. Those were just inconvenient side effects.

I opened the door to my room and was alone. Daniela was still at the party. I sat on my red velour blanket, staring at the wall. I wondered if Rachel would tell anyone. The room was spinning. After lying there for a while, I picked up the phone and called Jake in the Hat.

Fifteen minutes later, Jake in the Hat appeared at my door with his bouncy white-blond hair, coming from his own fraternity's party. I had unsatisfying sex with Jake in the Hat, then endured my twirling room until I could fall asleep. I was trying my best to convince myself I wasn't gay, but it wasn't working. Nobody can say I didn't try to be straight.

15

JAKE IN THE HAT

June–August, Sophomore Year

We tried to scrub black mold off the inside of our bathtub with bleach, without much success. Even after a few hours, the bathtub was still covered in a yellow film, with some black patches of mold we couldn't get off. We felt it was good enough for a shower, but there was no way any of us would take a bath in there. Chrissy and Laura, my sorority sisters, also attempted to clean the floors, toilet, and sink full of grime, hair, mildew, a few bugs, and who knows what else.

Our new room for the summer after our sophomore year cost only $300 a month. For this bargain price, we each got a single bed in one shared room, and a bathroom to share between the three of us. Jake in the Hat had hooked us up with this room on the bottom floor of the Kappa Sigma frat house. Many of his brothers were gone for the summer, and it was far cheaper than renting an apartment off campus.

I volunteered to take the top bunk. The bed was made of unfinished plywood that looked like an amateur woodshop project. I pictured a couple of frat boys scouring an old construction site for abandoned wood and hacking together the bunk bed in their front yard.

As I pulled off the sheet, dust and mold flew through the air. Stains covered the ratty, yellowing mattress. I found a red plastic cup full of someone's old tobacco chew spit on the corner of the mattress and gingerly picked it up, not able to avoid the pungent smell. I climbed down the wood ladder, holding the cup as far away from my body as I could.

I said to my new roommates, "Look what I found. A cup full of tobacco spit. This place is disgusting."

Chrissy was sweeping the floor. "Yeah, I can't believe anyone can live like this. It's so gross."

That first night, the old springs in the mattress squeaked as I climbed on. I had to duck my head to avoid hitting the ceiling. I saw what looked like cobwebs and cringed. Spiders were my nemesis. It felt like I was in a coffin, my small enclosed space covered on all sides with a threadbare tie-dye tapestry and the ceiling just a few inches above my face.

St. Louis summer temperatures often get into the 90s and, for at least a few weeks, the 100s. The high humidity and hot, stale air kept me awake for hours. I lay there on top of the sheets in boxers and a T-shirt, sweating. We had no air conditioning or fans. *This is what you get for $300.* It was going to be a long summer.

I spent the first part of the summer waiting for the public bus at 4 a.m. to make it to my 5 a.m. shift at the St. Louis Bread Company at the mall. I made minimum wage making sandwiches and serving pastries to customers. I didn't last long. Waking up that early was way too challenging.

Instead, I got a job at El Torito Grill, also in the St. Louis Galleria mall, which didn't open until 11 a.m. They wouldn't hire me as a server with no experience, so I started by bussing tables. Being from Texas, fajitas, queso, chips, and salsa were favorite foods, so I took full advantage of the free meals during my shifts. Unfortunately, this job did not last all summer. One evening a bunch of my friends and I decided to have dinner at the El Torito Grill where I worked. When the server came by to take our drink orders, I said "I'll have a strawberry daiquiri."

I had ordered these a few times at restaurants and, typically, when the server asked to see ID I'd say, "I just wanted a virgin strawberry daiquiri." Or, sometimes, when I received my drink there was no alcohol in it. Nobody in a restaurant had ever actually brought me a drink with alcohol in it before, although I was always hoping I could get away with it (I wasn't 21 yet).

This time, the server didn't flinch at all or ask me for my ID. We had seen each other at work before, but hadn't really spoken other than about work stuff as I was bussing his tables. When I received my drink, I was delighted and surprised to taste a real strawberry daiquiri with alcohol in it! The next time I came in for work they fired me for ordering alcohol when I was underage.

As a result, I moved on to my third job of the summer at the same mall. This time it was the Pasta House, an Italian chain restaurant similar to the Olive Garden. I was required to wear black pants, a button-down black shirt, and a tie. My favorite tie had a red, blue, and yellow plaid print, which I usually had to get Jake in the Hat to tie for me. I enjoyed picking out ties at the mall and loved how I looked in them. I felt at home in this uniform and looked forward to dressing for work. But once off work, the tie quickly came off. I had never seen a woman at my school (or anywhere other than at the Pasta House) wear a tie and wasn't comfortable enough in my own skin to be the first.

• • •

Jake in the Hat also lived in the Kappa Sigma frat house over the summer. We had been hooking up off and on since freshman year. We drank a lot and I did the "walk of shame" several times, hungover and slinking out of his frat house in the morning.

So, after a whole school year of questioning my sexuality, I did the least logical thing. When Jake in the Hat asked me to officially date him before the summer started, I said yes. The acceptance and kudos my sorority sisters gave me for dating a frat guy outweighed my doubts about whether I really wanted to be with him. Dating Jake in the Hat was the easy, acceptable route. It went with the flow of what was expected of me as a sorority girl, and gave me a boost in status.

But the pit in my stomach when I said "yes" haunted me throughout the whole summer. I tried obliterating a sinking feeling that I wasn't being true to myself by drinking and staying distracted, but the feelings followed me everywhere, every day.

Jake in the Hat lived in his single room in the basement of the KΣ house. The room looked like a dark closet, with a single bunk bed like mine, so close to the ceiling I couldn't sit up, and an old desk and dresser underneath. A tiny closet held a few button-down shirts. The best part of his room was the air-conditioning unit blowing frigid air right on his bed—a fantastic respite from the sweltering heat of my disgusting bunk, where I lay awake for hours drenched in sweat. I frequently slept with Jake—he'd crank his A/C up to high until the tiny room felt like a refreshing refrigerator.

One night, he and I met some people from his frat and some of my sorority sisters at a pub across the street from campus. We all got very drunk and Jake in the Hat and I decided to go to Forest Park, right across the street from campus. We drove around and around in the large park until we found a deserted area with trees, where we pulled over and started to fool around. We kept bumping into the steering wheel and felt cramped, so we got out.

We stumbled into a secluded area with trees. There were tons of mosquitoes biting us, and it was dark except for the moon and stars overhead and an occasional car passing by.

All the sudden, a huge blinding light shone directly at us. Jake in the Hat stopped and got up on his knees, looking into the blinding light. "What the fuck?!"

Blinded by the brightness, we couldn't see anything. We heard a car door opening, some crunching on the ground, and a deep voice say, "This is the police. You can't be out here at night."

We fumbled around, trying to find our clothes in the grass.

The policeman continued, "I need to see your license and registration. Now."

I got into the passenger side of the car without saying anything, and heard the officer tell Jake he needed to get a Missouri license, now that he lived here. I couldn't believe he didn't try to give him a DUI. We were both drunk and neither of us were 21. We got lucky.

That summer, I spent my days working and my nights sleeping with Jake in his icy room. By the end of the summer, I felt perpetually annoyed with Jake and wrote about it a lot in my journal. His argumentativeness, lack of awareness of his feelings and inability to communicate them, and the way he bragged about things I didn't care about, like making a big welt on a guy's neck with a frozen paintball, irritated me. His room now felt stifling and we rarely spent time there any more or fooled around.

In my sweltering bed, I repeatedly replayed a memory of Peyton, a sorority sister, while on spring break with her and two of my other sorority sisters in Florida. We had been watching a disturbing movie, *Twin Peaks,* and during a scary scene Peyton had tightly grabbed my arm and put her head on my shoulder, pulling in close to me. A rush of adrenaline had overwhelmed my body and I instantly felt an attraction to her. My senses were electrified whenever I was around her for the rest of the trip. That summer, I also often thought about Alex's smile, the fleeting moments when she touched my arm, her lingering hugs, and her laughter.

The further into the summer it got, the more Jake in the Hat annoyed me and the less time I spent with him. Thoughts of Peyton and Alex intensified and consumed me. I became less adept at repressing my fantasies and started to relish the rare moments I had to myself, so that I could let my thoughts go where they wanted to.

After the summer ended, I moved into a three-bedroom apartment on campus with Daniela, Dawn, and Jackie from my sorority. At the beginning of junior year, I told Jake I no longer wanted to date him. I just couldn't force myself to be intimate with him anymore. Although I struggled with the decision for a few weeks, I didn't cry over it. Instead I felt a sense of relief, like I could stop paddling upstream. I was exhausted from trying so hard.

PART THREE

JUNIOR YEAR

16

CRUSH

September, Junior Year

It started out like any other Thursday night. Four of my sorority sisters joined my three roommates and me in our on-campus apartment for amaretto sours, fuzzy navels, and shots of tequila. Then the seven of us, all Thetas, walked to the Student Union and descended the stairs to the Pub, the bar located right next to the Rat, where I had met Alex months ago. A sea of 16-ounce red plastic cups filled the bar. Everything inside—the floors, chairs, tables, and bar—was a weathered dark wood. The low ceilings, lack of windows, and humidity from so many students packed in such a small space created a claustrophobic atmosphere. The overhead lights shone brightly, casting a yellow hue on everything.

Students stuffed inside, shoulder to shoulder. We could barely move. Fraternity letters covered T-shirts and sweatshirts and baseball caps, but no sorority letters could be found. This was not because the Pub wasn't packed with sorority girls; on the contrary, members of the seven different sororities each filled different pockets of the bar—talking, laughing, drinking, and flirting with frat guys. Greek letters of the sororities were absent because of the golden rule of the four S's: sorority girls didn't need to wear their letters when sleeping or showering. We were forbidden to wear our letters when having sex or not sober.

The seven of us pushed through the crowd to the bar. Other sorority sisters and guys scattered in the crowd waved to us. Seven Bud Lights slid across the bar. The Pub didn't require ID, and few of us were 21 yet.

As we navigated toward the Theta table, my shoulders pressed against bodies. Twenty of us tried to squeeze around a table meant for ten. I saw Rachel across the table. We hadn't spoken again about my revelation next to the tennis courts at the end of last year. She never checked in on me to see how I was doing. It felt like as long as it was unspoken, I could continue as if our talk had never happened: pretend to be straight and try to fit in. An uneasiness was growing inside me and I felt like an imposter with a secret to hide.

I tried shaking off these feelings as we played Quarters, trying to bounce quarters into empty cups. When I lost, I attempted to drink my beer without knocking over other cups or elbowing someone else's beer out of their hands.

After a while, Daniela turned to me and said, "Hey, you want to go over to the Rat? The band starts at 10."

"Yeah, let's go."

Daniela, a couple of my sorority sisters, and I said our goodbyes and made our way through the crowd. We pushed through the underground tunnel that led to the Rat. An amateur band I'd never heard of was playing break-your-eardrums alternative rock music that reverberated in my body. The dim lighting transformed the Rat into a nightclub atmosphere, a sharp contrast to the bright lights of the Pub. We wove through the hordes of students standing and swaying to the music. I felt some cold beer splash on my arm, soaking my sleeve.

We found a place to stop in the middle of the swarm. I caught brief glimpses of the scruffy band by standing on my tiptoes and moving my head side to side to peer between people. I moved to the beat of the drums and took the remaining sips of my beer, trying to ignore the off-tune yelling of the singer and lack of any identifiable melody. I couldn't understand anything they were saying.

I felt someone squeeze my right upper arm and turned around.

Alex stood six inches from my face. She said "Hey, Kristin!"

My heart felt like it was pounding to the beat of the music. I stood there frozen, staring at her. She smiled warmly. I couldn't hold back my smile.

I managed to snap out of it enough to mumble "Hey." The corners of her mouth turned up into a wider smile. My arm tingled as she gave my arm another squeeze, then slowly released her hand and made her way back through the crowd. Wearing jeans and a black jacket, she strode through the throng of people. I watched her until she disappeared, then continued to stare at the space she had just vacated, still feeling the touch of her fingers on my arm.

I heard "Who was that?" from one of my sorority sisters.

I abruptly swung my head around to look at her. It took me a moment to process what she was saying. Then I felt my face flush and stammered, "Oh, um, uh, just someone from one of my classes."

"Oh, okay." She turned to the band again.

As I stood there, thoughts raced through my mind. *Do any of my sisters know Alex is gay? Did they see her squeeze my arm? Did they notice me smiling at her?*

I turned back to the band, but all I could think about was Alex. I had been thinking about her all summer and this was the first time I had seen her this year. Conflicting thoughts swirled. *Maybe I should go talk to her? No, I can't. What would I even say? "You're so hot and I have a crush on you"...? "Will you make out with me?" And what if my sisters saw us talking?* I fidgeted with my cup, then started to bite it at its edges.

We got more beers. My head buzzed. I couldn't get Alex out of my head. *Should I go find her? I think I have to.*

After staring mindlessly at the band and obsessing, I told Daniela I had to go pee, then left before she had a chance to come with me or make it a group excursion.

Making my way through the crowd, I reached the brightness of the student union and looked for Alex. I spotted her around the corner from the water fountain, talking to another girl. Looking at the beer I held in my hands, I thought, *Liquid courage, don't fail me now.* I was out of breath, like I had just run a sprint. I took another swig of beer, breathed in deeply, then moved toward them.

When I got to them, I said, "Hey Alex!"

They both looked over. Alex looked surprised. She said, "Hey Kristin. How's it goin'?"

"Um, good. Yeah. Can I talk to you for a minute?"

"Sure," she said in an upbeat tone.

I took my last gulp of beer. "Um, in private?"

Alex looked at the other girl, who nodded and took off, then she looked around. "You wanna go over there?" She pointed to a corner where nobody was.

I followed her, scanning the crowd for people I knew. I saw a couple seniors from my sorority, but they were busy chatting with others and didn't seem to notice me. Alex stopped and looked at me, smiling. I couldn't help but smile back awkwardly.

"So, what's goin' on? How was your summer?" she asked.

"It was good. I stayed here and worked. Nothing too exciting."

We made small talk for a few minutes about our summers. At some point I noticed my hand holding my empty beer cup was shaking, so I put it down on the stairs.

Alex touched my arm and asked, "Is everything okay?"

In a shaky voice I said, "Well, kind of. Well, not really, exactly. I just don't even know how to say this, but I've been thinking about things a lot over the summer. I mean, I still feel like I might not be straight, but I haven't done anything about it yet."

Alex listened intently and didn't say anything. She leaned in to hear me; I was talking quietly, so no one else could hear. She was just inches away from me, which made me uncomfortable, but also excited—like I was skydiving and about to jump out of the airplane. Taking a deep breath, I started again.

"So, I thought about you a lot over the summer." I held my breath.

"Oh yeah? You did?" She flashed a sly smile.

"Yeah." I paused, then started again. "Yeah, I did. A lot." She moved in a little closer, but didn't say anything.

I fidgeted with my pockets. Unable to make eye contact, I said, "Well, what I'm trying to say is that I really like you. You know what I mean?" I brought my eyes up and looked at her.

She placed her hand on my upper arm and squeezed slightly and said, "Yeah, I know what you mean." She paused, keeping her hand on my arm.

I looked down at the floor again. "I'm so embarrassed."

"Don't be. Please don't be at all."

I didn't know what to say or do next. Luckily, she continued with "Do you wanna come back to my room and talk some more? Just hang out where it's quieter?"

My stomach started to do back flips with anticipation of kissing Alex. I managed to mumble, "Um, sure. Yeah, okay. That sounds good."

As I started to follow Alex out of the Student Union, I wondered how I would explain my disappearance to my sisters. I told myself they would probably be too drunk to notice anything for a while. When they did notice, they might assume I went home with a guy, was hanging out with some other sisters, or that I went over to the Kappa Sig house for the after party. Or, they might think they just couldn't find me because it was so crowded. I looked around, pretty sure nobody I knew would notice me slipping out.

We walked out into the crisp night air. Clusters of students lingered outside, smoking and drinking. It felt like it took an eternity, walking on the dark path across campus to her dorm. We entered the lobby then took the elevator up to her floor. My hands were trembling as she unlocked her door, so I stuffed them into the pockets of my jeans. She held the door open for me and I walked into her room. She followed closely, placing her hand on the small of my back.

Her tiny single room contained a bunk bed with a futon couch below it. A small desk and chair, a tiny dresser, and a tiny closet filled the rest of the space. I sat on the chair and turned it to face the center of the room.

She sat on one end of the futon. She smiled at me. "Why don't you come and sit next to me?" When I didn't say anything or move, she patted the space on the futon next to her. "It'll be more comfortable."

My heart sped up. "Okay."

I slowly got up and joined her on the opposite end of the futon, as far away from her as possible. I couldn't really look at her, but I could see that she had turned her body to face mine. She inched a little closer to me, then placed her left hand on my right knee. I shivered slightly. When I finally looked up at her, I saw she was smiling. She inched closer. I turned slightly toward her, but my hands were at my sides. She leaned in toward me and we were merely inches apart, face to face. The clean scent of her hair mixed with cigarette smoke. A kiss after so many hours spent fantasizing about her? She was like a powerful magnet I couldn't control—and didn't want to.

Suddenly, her phone rang loudly. She reflexively jumped up and said, "Sorry, I've got to take this call." She picked up the phone. "Hello?" She paused, listening, then turned to me and said, "I'm so sorry, but do you mind stepping outside for just a minute? I'm really sorry."

I walked out into the hallway and leaned against the wall. I hovered, waiting for her to finish, wondering why she needed to take the call and what it was about. After a few minutes, she popped her head out and looked for me.

"Hey, I'm so sorry about that. Come back in." She motioned for me to join her.

When I came back in, she wasn't smiling like before. She sat back down on the futon and I sat next to her, just like earlier, but she didn't lean in, or put her hand back on my knee. She looked at me with a slightly pained look and didn't immediately say anything. After a few moments, she said, "That was my girlfriend on the phone. She's on a semester abroad in London."

I felt like I'd been slapped in the face. I blurted out, "You have a girlfriend?!"

"Yeah. I'm so sorry. We can't do this. I'm so sorry I brought you here."

My face burned.

She continued, "Let me walk you back to your place."

At the front steps of my building we stopped, and she said, "I'm really sorry about tonight." She leaned in and gave me a tight, lingering hug. I felt her breasts against mine and electricity moved through my skin.

After she let go, I said, "Yeah, me too."

"Okay, I'll see you around…maybe at GLBA or something." She turned to go.

It was about midnight when I trudged into my apartment and flopped into bed. My roommates were probably all still at the Kappa Sig after party. I was alone. I lay in bed staring at the ceiling.

I'm such an idiot. Disappointment was crushing me. This particular rejection stung like none I'd ever had. With guys I could take it or leave it. This felt altogether different. The power of Alex's gaze and touch created an intensity of longing I hadn't felt since those warm summer nights at Six Flags with Brandi. Only later did I feel proud of myself that I told Alex how I felt. But now, it just stung to my core.

17

GLBA

October, Junior Year

I walked briskly in the dark, pulling my khaki Eddie Bauer jacket tighter to block the breeze. William had told me exactly where to go, but said it could be hard to find.

I arrived near the base of the stairs that led up to frat row, where we had caught the buses to Jake in the Hat's semiformal freshman year. Two years ago, I had wobbled down the stairs in heels and a dress, thrilled to attend my first Greek date party. Now, I stood alone, staring at a dark brick building, unsure what I wanted to do next.

William had finally talked me into attending a GLBA (Gay, Lesbian, Bisexual Alliance) meeting, after I struggled with the decision for months. The group was secret and mostly invisible to the rest of campus. Meetings were held every Friday night from 7–9 p.m., in the basement of an on-campus apartment building—unlike other clubs, which had legitimate on-campus homes.

I found what looked like the back door William had described. I needed a key to get in, but didn't have one. William had said I would either need to wait until someone else went in and go in after them or knock on the window of the basement where the meeting was held, so someone could come and let me in. I looked around for the window he was talking about. There were a few, and I couldn't see in, so couldn't be sure.

Instead of knocking on a bunch of different windows, I walked back to the door. It was 7:05 p.m. After a few minutes, a guy came to the door and started to open it. I stood, scared to go in and unable to move. *Will I be welcome even though I don't know if I'm gay and have never been with a woman? Are they going to judge me for being in a sorority?*

He went in and the door shut behind him. I still couldn't move. I scanned the walkways, hoping nobody I knew would walk by. I waited a few more minutes, but nobody else went in the door. It was now 7:13 p.m.

Maybe I should just go home and go to the frat party instead. As I was leaving my apartment about 20 minutes before, Dawn and Jackie, my roommates and sorority sisters, were watching TV, and Daniela was getting ready in the bathroom. I stood in the kitchen with a glass of water, staring at the back of Jackie and Dawn's heads on the couch. My hand started to shake, so I put the glass on the counter. I knew I would be late if I didn't slip out now—but the only door outside was past the living room, so they would see me if I left.

I paused a few more moments, then spoke to the back of their heads. "Hey guys, I don't think I'll be able to go with you to the party. I'm meeting up with Jake in the Hat, but I will catch up with you guys later."

Dawn turned around and said, "I thought you guys weren't dating anymore."

Jake in the Hat was the only person I could think of that they wouldn't check up on or know what he was doing. "Yeah, but we still hang out sometimes."

This was marginally true. We had drunkenly hooked up a couple of times so far during the school year.

I don't think they suspected anything. Jake in the Hat better not go to that party or I'm screwed.

Back at the basement window, I started to worry that I would be awkwardly late at this point. I walked over to the ground-level window and stood there for a moment, then knocked quickly but not too loudly. I walked over to the door and waited some more. 7:15 p.m. Nothing. *Crap.*

I knocked again—this time more loudly. *Maybe I should just leave now before anyone answers. This is my chance.* I waited in front of the window, but kept my eye on the door.

Finally, the door creaked open and a guy that looked like an accountant opened the door and peeked out. *Is he from the meeting? What should I say? What if I say "GLBA" and he doesn't know what I'm talking about?*

"Are you here for the meeting?"

"Uh, yes."

"Come on in." He held the door open as I approached. "I'm Matt." He was wearing acid-washed jeans, an '80s patterned sweater, and tennis shoes.

I hesitated, then said "Hi, I'm Kristin."

I followed him through a barren concrete corridor in the basement. We passed the laundry room and I could hear the washer and dryer clanking away. We arrived at a door, and he opened it.

Questions rattled about in my mind. *What if someone finds out I attended the meeting? What if I see someone there from a fraternity or sorority and they tell others?*

Will all the women have short hair, piercings, and tattoos, and not shave their legs and armpits? Will all the gay guys be effeminate, wear fashionable clothes, and have a lisp? If so, I definitely wouldn't fit in with my J. Crew rugby shirt, long blond hair, no tattoos, no piercings.

We walked into a room bathed in harsh fluorescent lighting. About a dozen people sat on a dingy orange couch, two old wooden chairs, and rugs on the concrete floor. A sparsely populated bookshelf against one wall held a few books and flyers. The freezing air led me to believe the heating didn't work, if there was any in the basement to begin with. William sat on a greenish rug and Alex in one of the chairs. At the sight of Alex, my heart sunk, thinking about our previous encounter.

Everyone turned to look as we walked in. Matt said, "Everyone, this is Kristin."

I waved weakly and said "Hi," then squeezed in next to William. Matt sat in the chair next to Alex. My heart pumped loudly. I hadn't talked to Alex since the night I went back to her dorm room. But what made me even more insecure than Alex was the presence of all the gay people in the room. *Will I fit in? Do I even belong here?*

William leaned over and whispered, "You made it! I thought you weren't going to come."

I looked around. A slightly overweight, unshaven guy sat on the other side of William. A pale woman with dreadlocks wearing overalls sat on the couch; next to her, a preppy-looking guy with a button-down plaid polo shirt tucked into his jeans, and topsiders. The rest of the group looked nothing like the coiffed pastel uniformity of my sorority either. Mesmerized, I sat on the ratty rug, picking nervously at the corners, and absorbed the scene.

Alex looked at Unshaven Guy and said, "So, we were talking about dating and PDA. You were about to say something?"

Unshaven Guy said, "So, I'm dating this guy I met at Probe and I like him, but we keep fighting about PDA. He's older and has been out for a long time, so he feels really comfortable with PDA. The other night we went out to a movie and he tried to hold my hand. I just couldn't do it. I heard some guy got beat up right outside Probe one night and had to be taken to the hospital. I mean, if we're not safe outside of a gay bar, where are we safe?"

Dreadlocks said, "I understand about needing to be cautious and paying attention to your surroundings. You obviously don't want to be making out in some straight ghetto at night when you're alone— but at the same time, if others are uncomfortable, fuck them. Straight people can make out and hold hands everywhere, why can't we?"

Unshaven Guy responded, "That's great and everything in theory but I don't want to get beat up. I've heard too many stories about how the police don't protect you and even sometimes bash gay people themselves."

Preppy Guy chimed in, "I don't want to make people feel uncomfortable with PDA. If there are kids around, I don't think it's appropriate to expose them to gay people kissing. Parents may not want their kids to see that."

Dreadlocks said, "Are you serious? You're worried about how parents feel? What about how we feel? We should be able to enjoy affection like they do. It's not fair."

A blond-haired guy with glasses and a big nose shyly said, "I wouldn't hold hands with anyone in public. Once my boyfriend was standing close to me when we were at Blockbuster and some guys looked at us with disgust and one yelled 'Faggots. Get a fucking room!' then stormed off. I can't imagine holding hands in public."

Alex said, "Has anyone held hands with someone of the opposite sex in public?"

Dreadlocks was the only person to raise her hand.

I thought about my make-out sessions next to my high school locker with James. People would whistle and smile at us—making out made me cooler. Having a boyfriend in high school made me feel noticed and accepted. I wanted people to know. When my older boyfriend, Shaun, picked me up in his Pontiac Sunfire after school, I wanted everyone to see him. PDA had always felt like something to be proud of, proof that the person really liked me. Girls were proud to flaunt their boyfriends in public—straight PDA gained you status. Hearing about how gay PDA was the exact opposite—opening you up to ridicule, ostracism, and violence—made me sad and scared.

The room became quiet. After an awkward silence, Matt asked, "Has anyone here ever been called names because they were gay?"

Everyone raised their hands except for me and one other girl in a red blouse. I felt people looking at me. I smiled awkwardly, but didn't say anything.

Matt said, "What kinds of names have you been called?"

"Dyke, lezzie."

"Faggot."

"Fudge Packer."

"Carpet Muncher."

"Fagatron."

"Fairy."

Matt then asked, "What do you do when you get called names?"

William said, "I usually just try to ignore them."

Unshaven Guy said, "Yeah, me too. I don't really say anything. I don't know what to say."

Dreadlocks was the only person that said they would confront the person. "Sometimes I'll say, 'So? What's your problem?' I feel like I have to say something."

After this subject died down, Matt asked the group, "Is there anything you guys want to talk about?"

Glasses Guy said "Dating." After a pause, he said, "Where do you guys meet people to date?"

Preppy Guy said, "Bars. I meet guys all the time at clubs and bars. I mostly like to go to Fallout, Probe, and the Loading Zone."

Dreadlocks said, "I've dated a couple of girls from the LBQ group on campus."

Red Blouse Girl said, "What's LBQ?"

Dreadlocks said, "That's the women's lesbian, bisexual, and questioning group. They meet once every few weeks."

Unshaven Guy said, "The guy I'm kind of dating now I met at a gay party."

Am I the only person here who hasn't dated someone of the same sex? I hope they don't ask me anything. Maybe I shouldn't be here, since I don't know if I'm gay. I was the only person who didn't say anything during the meeting.

At the end of the meeting Alex said, "Okay, everyone, so we're going to go to Fallout tonight as usual!" Looking at me, she said, "For those of you that haven't been, it's a gay dance club downtown. Lots of cute girls and boys there! It's a lot of fun. You should all come out."

William turned to me. "Do you want to come? I'm going."

"Um, I have to meet my roommates at this frat party they're going to tonight."

"Are you sure? It's really fun!"

"Uh, maybe another time. I just feel really uncomfortable. I mean, I'm not even sure if I should be here."

"Okay, another time. I'm glad you came." He smiled.

"Plus, I really don't want to have to talk to Alex. I want to get out of here before she comes over." Alex was talking to some of the other people, and I snuck out. The thought of going to the frat party was unappealing, but that's what my sorority sisters and I did every weekend.

When I arrived at the party, Daniela first asked, "How was Jake in the Hat? What did you guys do?"

I flinched, suddenly wanting to tell Daniela where I really had been. I looked at my best friend's welcoming smile and paused. I thought about all the good times we'd had together over the last two years, studying together, bonding over tough crew workouts, processing hookups and relationships with boys. She was the best friend I had ever had. The thought of harming our relationship stopped me in my tracks.

To Daniela's question about where I was, I said, "Nothing much. We just hung out at the house." I was disappointed in myself for not being honest.

At the frat party, I drank beer after beer and had meaningless conversations about boys and parties. All the while I was thinking about the GLBA meeting, Alex, the girl wearing the red blouse, and the basement with the orange couch. I chain-smoked about a half pack of Marlboro Reds. I felt strangely alone even amidst the large crowd of people.

As I walked home, I felt caught between two worlds, not fully belonging to either.

18

SARAH

October, Junior Year

At the next GLBA meeting, I sat on the green rug between William and the quiet girl who'd worn the red blouse the week before. Most of the same people were there.

Toward the end of the meeting Alex announced, "We'd like to have a GLBA dance on campus in a couple of weeks. We're planning to have a DJ from KWUR bring some music in. You can invite friends too. Can anyone help Matt and me put flyers up on campus?"

Daniela and I had decided we wanted to be DJs at KWUR, Wash U's student-run alternative music station. We applied and secured the dreaded 3–5 a.m. timeslot. I always had trouble deciding whether to sleep for a couple of hours before the 3 a.m. shift or to skip sleeping until 5 a.m., after the shift ended—neither option really worked. We played music by female singers that nobody listened to—it was the middle of the night, after all—and I quit after a couple of weeks.

In the musty basement, nobody answered Alex's request to hang flyers. "Come on, guys. It won't take that long. We don't have access to all the dorms and buildings, so can't get flyers up everywhere. We need your help."

Glasses Guy said, "I'd like to help, but I'm just not out yet."

William said, "Yeah, me neither. I'm sorry."

Matt jumped in with, "Who is out on campus?"

Dreadlocks said, "Well, I'm out to my roommate, but that's it. I don't really like to label myself."

Matt looked at Preppy Guy and asked, "What about you, Barrett?"

Barrett said, "I'm out to a few close friends, but I don't want everyone to know. If I put flyers up people are going to know."

Matt then looked at the quiet girl next to me and said, "What about you, Sarah?"

She said, "No, sorry. I'm not out at all."

I stayed silent. The only sound was from the clothes dryer, muffled by the wall. Everyone was too scared; nobody volunteered.

As everyone was milling around after, I turned to Sarah and asked, "Are you going to Fallout?"

"No, are you?"

"No." I paused, then said, "Have you ever been?"

"No. I've actually never been to a gay bar." She brushed her long brown hair behind her ear and smiled sheepishly.

"Me neither." I smiled back. I wasn't sure what to say next, so I tried to leverage the small talk skills I'd acquired when prepping for sorority rush. Striking up conversations with people I barely knew was a learned skill for me.

"What year are you?" I asked.

"I'm a freshman. What about you?"

"I'm a junior." I paused. "So, how long have you been coming to GLBA? This is only my second time."

"I've been to most meetings since the start of the year. When I started Wash U I looked for a group like this."

"Nice." I stammered. I didn't want her to leave just yet, so I asked her another question. "Where are you from?"

"I'm from upstate New York. My parents live in Rochester. You?"

"I bet it's cold there. I've never been. I'm from Austin, Texas. It never even snows there."

I felt William tap on my shoulder. "Hey, I'm going to Fallout with everyone. You want to come?"

"No, I promised to go to a party with some of my sorority sisters."

"Okay, well, have fun. But you should really come out with us sometime!"

"Yeah, I know. Maybe." I smiled at him.

At this point, everyone was standing up and chatting and a few people had already left. I turned back to Sarah. We were both still sitting on the floor.

"You're in a sorority?" she asked.

"Yeah, I know that seems a little weird."

"Well, yeah, a little. Do they know you're gay?"

My hands started to sweat and suddenly I felt tongue-tied. I looked down and pulled at the rug where it was unravelling. I could feel her looking at me and waiting for an answer. I finally managed to make partial eye contact and say, "Um, well, I don't actually know that I'm gay. I think I might be bisexual but I'm not really sure."

She spoke confidently, saying, "Okay, well, I'm pretty sure I'm gay but I'm not 100 percent sure either."

"Really?" I asked.

"Yeah, I've never actually been with a woman before." She smiled at me bashfully.

I was too embarrassed to say I hadn't either. *Time to change the subject.* "Um, where do you live?"

"I live in Liggett. Where are you?"

"I live in an on-campus apartment." I noticed people starting to leave, so I said, "I've actually got to go meet my friends. Are you coming to next week's meeting?"

"Yes."

"Me too. So, I'll see you then?"

"Yes, for sure." She grinned.

A spark of excitement lit me up.

• • •

Sarah's dorm was located completely across campus from where my apartment was. How would I explain why I was in the area? I didn't want her to know I'd walked 20 minutes across campus just in the hopes of seeing her.

I waited until about 8 p.m., when I figured she'd be back from dinner and might be hanging out in her room. Arriving at the three-story freshman dorm, I had to wait a few minutes until someone who lived there let me in.

In the lobby I asked a random student, "Do you know where Sarah lives?" I didn't know her last name.

"No, don't know a Sarah."

In the common area on the first floor, nervous energy coursed through my body. I had been thinking about her since the last GLBA meeting and, despite my fear of rejection, my feet pulled me up the stairwell. The worn linoleum stairs creaked. I randomly picked a floor and stepped out onto the dirty carpet in the hallway. I assessed the scene from the end of the hallway. A few doors were open and I poked my head in the first one I came to. A skater-looking guy sat on the floor with a pizza box next to him. I asked, "Do you know where Sarah's room is?"

"Yeah, just a couple of rooms down on this side."

I walked out of his room, took a deep breath, and stood for a couple of minutes, leaning against the wall. I started to chew on my fingernails. *It'll be fine. I'm just casually stopping by. No big deal. Totally cool.*

I took another deep breath, then slowly inched a couple doors down to an open door. I timidly looked in, but just saw two guys. "Sorry, wrong room."

I inched along the wall again until I reached the next open door. I slowly peered in and saw Sarah sitting on the floor with a woman. They were leaning against their single beds on opposite sides of the room, massive textbooks open on their laps. Neither noticed me.

I shoved my hands in my pockets, to stop biting my fingernails, and said "Hey, Sarah."

They both looked up. Sarah looked surprised at first, then a smile arrived on her face.

"I was meeting someone at the Bear's Den and thought I'd stop by. You said you lived in Liggett."

"Hey!" She paused briefly then said "Kristin, this is my roommate, Shipra."

"Hey." Shipra nodded a hello. Papers and books littered the floor and their beds.

I stood in the doorway and asked, "What are you guys up to?"

Sarah said, "Just studying. Biology."

"Are you guys pre-med?"

They both said yes. About one third of freshman at Washington University at that time started out pre-med—it's a top-notch medical school. However, most students didn't finish the grueling pre-med coursework and never applied to medical school.

Sarah said, "What major are you?"

"Psych. And I'm probably going to minor in art history or women's studies."

After a moment of silence, Shipra turned to Sarah and said, "I'm gonna ask Lola about the problem set we're stuck on. I'll be back in a bit."

After Shipra left, I turned to Sarah. "So, you said you're from upstate New York. What did you like to do there?" I was still standing awkwardly in the doorway.

"Come in and sit down," she said. She cleared away some papers next to her.

"Yeah, okay. Thanks." I sat in a chair a few feet away from her.

"I was on the swim team in high school," she replied. "That's how I spent most of my free time."

She seemed short to be a swimmer. I'd joined Wash U's rowing team my sophomore year, but I was too short to get really good. Although I loved the camaraderie, the challenge, and rowing in the Creve Coeur Lake on beautiful fall afternoons, I didn't last long. It became clear that the three-hour practices six days a week, especially on Saturday mornings, were really cutting into my social life. I quit right before spring break, so I could spend that time in Florida with three of my sorority sisters instead of at rowing practice all week.

One of the things that had kept me on the team that long was our coach, Regan, who I later discovered was a lesbian. Recently out of college and in phenomenal shape from being a serious rower,

Regan had long blond hair and bronzed skin that glittered in the sun. I felt intimidated and tongue-tied around her. While riding beside us in her motorboat, she often screamed "Stop pulling crabs!"— always with a smile. It's called "catching a crab" when your oar gets caught in the water because you put it in at an incorrect angle. If this happens, the whole boat can come to a roaring stop and start turning sideways. Our entire boat tipped over a few times, which is unnerving because your feet are buckled in and you have to quickly unhook them while underwater.

I said, "Cool. I played soccer my senior year. When I was really young, I tried diving and was practicing back dives when I didn't jump far enough out and scraped my back on the diving board. Someone had to jump in and pull me out. I can't do back dives anymore." I babble when I'm nervous, going off on random tangents.

After some small talk, I got up the nerve to ask, "So you said that you thought you were gay, but have never been with a woman before?"

"Yeah, I think I've known for a while. I didn't tell anyone in high school. I just haven't had the opportunity to act on it. It seems like it will be much easier here to meet someone and come out."

"Yeah, I guess so. I can't imagine anyone being out in high school. There was definitely nobody gay in any of my high schools. At least nobody was out."

"Yeah, me neither." Sarah paused, then asked, "So, have you dated a woman before?"

Deep breaths. Deep breaths.

I mumbled softly, "Um, no I haven't."

She leaned in. "Oh, I guess I assumed you had."

"No. Um, I'm just starting to figure things out. I've always dated guys in the past, but I just don't know. I mean, I think I might be bi."

I felt my face flush and burn. *Can she tell I'm blushing?* She smiled at me. After a few more minutes, her roommate came back in.

I said, "You know, maybe we could hang out another time, or if I'm in the area again I could stop by."

"Oh, yes. That would be great." She smiled broadly. I thought her eyes sparkled a little. As I started to leave and looked back at her, my shoulder hit the side of the doorway. *So embarrassing.*

19

DOUBLE DATE

October, Junior Year

On my cow-print futon, I replayed my conversation with Sarah over and over. I thought about her sparkly eyes, full of life. I thought about the way she looked at me, fully present. I scribbled quickly in my journal, words describing Sarah pouring onto the pages and energy coursing through my body despite the late hour. I fantasized about sitting next to her at our next GLBA meeting, feeling her warm presence and learning more about her. *Should I stop by her dorm again?*

Across the room, Daniela plopped down on her multicolored bedspread next to an array of books, notebooks, and pencils. Her slightly wavy dark brown hair extended below her shoulders, onto her green Wash U sweatshirt. A darkness washed over me as I thought about the new secret I had been keeping from her. My chest pounded. Engrossed in her book, she never looked up.

"Hey, Daniela," I said.

Her gaze stayed on her book. "Yeah?"

I closed the notebook on my lap and shoved it to the side. "Um, uh, there's something I wanted to tell you."

As she continued to stare into her book, there was a long pause before she answered. "Okay."

"Um, yeah. Well, you know how I've been gone on Friday nights lately?"

She looked up. "Yeah?"

"Well, I've been going to meetings with William to this group on campus called the Gay, Lesbian, Bisexual Alliance and I met someone there that I think I might kinda like."

The corners of her mouth turned up into an almost imperceptible smile. Daniela was Catholic and although I'd never seen her go to church, I'd braced myself for a negative reaction. While she hadn't seemed particularly fazed when I told her I thought I might be bisexual in a recent conversation, that's very different than having a crush on a girl and potentially acting on the feelings. I felt my shoulders relax a little.

The door to our room was open, but the doors to both Jackie's and Dawn's single rooms were closed. Despite this, I continued to speak quietly. "There's this girl I met at the group, Sarah. She's a freshman and totally cute. I was completely petrified, but I went over to her dorm last night to see her."

"Wow, really? What happened?"

I said, "Nothing really. We just talked. I don't know. I'll probably see her at the next GLBA meeting though."

"Do you want to go out with her?"

"Um, I mean, maybe. You mean like on a date?"

"Yeah. Maybe you should ask her out."

My fingernails on the futon-cover sounded like a zipper going back and forth. After a few moments I looked up again and said, "It's weird, 'cause with guys it's like you don't really have to do anything. They're supposed to make the first move and ask you out."

Daniela leaned forward and spoke excitedly. "Maybe you could go to a movie. Wait, I've got an idea. We could go on a double date! You and Sarah and me and Simon!"

Daniela's enthusiasm filled me with relief. I had finally fully let my secret out. Her excitement and support solidified her place as my best friend for years to come.

• • •

Sitting on peeling red vinyl, inches from Sarah, I felt electric when she turned and smiled at me. Did we see *The Adventures of Priscilla, Queen of the Desert*? Drag queens parading around the desert were probably too racy for it to even be playing in St. Louis. Would we have seen *The Shawshank Redemption*? That seems a bit serious for college students. *Interview with the Vampire* seems the most likely, but I honestly don't remember because I was so focused on Sarah.

Sounds of people sucking soda through straws and the crunching of popcorn filled the air. The lights dimmed and the movie started.

The crisp clean scent of Sarah's shampoo wafted my way, mingling with the smell of buttered popcorn. I felt the warmth of her shoulder next to mine. Engrossed in the screen, Daniela and Simon held hands to my left. *Should I try to hold hands with Sarah?* When I wanted Shaun, the night stocker, to hold my hand, I placed my hand on the edge of my leg, as close to him as possible. He inevitably moved his arm off the armrest and took it.

The armrest between Sarah and me was empty. My hands sat

together in my lap, and so did hers. *Does she want to hold hands? Does she even know this is a date? What will happen if I try to hold her hand? Will she reject me? Will anyone see us holding hands? If they do, will they call us names? What if she just wants to be friends? How will I know?*

I saw her move out of the corner of my eye. Her left hand now rested on her left leg. *Does that mean she wants me to take her hand?* I wiped my hands on my jeans and placed my right arm on the armrest, then inched closer to her.

I looked over at Daniela and she was leaning her head against Simon's shoulder, holding his hand. His arm was around her shoulders. *Maybe I should try putting my arm around her like guys do in movies?* I could stretch my arms up over my head, then nonchalantly place one arm around Sarah's shoulder. But that seemed more cheesy than suave. And if my arm was around Sarah's shoulder, that would be even more obvious than holding hands. If someone yelled "dykes" at us that would make for the worst date ever. She'd probably never go out with me again.

I suddenly noticed that our shoulders were slightly touching. *Did she just inch toward me or did I imagine that?* My fingers tingled and my heart thumped. I moved ever so lightly to the right, so my shoulder was pressed more solidly against her. She didn't move away. Her left hand was on her knee, just inches from mine. *Should I try? What if she pulls away?* I would be mortified.

The movie ended and the lights came on. I hadn't had the guts to try to hold her hand.

Before Sarah got out of the car, we shared a prolonged hug, her large breasts pressed against mine, her arms wrapped tightly around my body and mine around hers. I couldn't take my eyes off her as she walked to her dorm. I was more drawn to her than I'd ever been to anyone. I couldn't stop thinking about her.

20

FIRST KISS

October, Junior Year

I followed Sarah down the stairs to the first-floor common area of her dorm. She walked toward the back and around a corner, then took a right into a small doorway. The room had no windows, a ratty brown couch, and four washer and dryer units. The scent of sweaty gym socks and Febreze fabric softener hung in the air. A white plastic laundry basket sat atop the units. Down here, we wouldn't need to worry about keeping Sarah's roommate awake.

Sarah sat on one end of the couch and I sat on the other. She folded one leg under her, to face me. I did the same, facing her. Almost immediately after we sat down, a girl with a pink sorority sweatshirt walked in and started pulling laundry out of the dryer and stuffing it into her laundry basket unfolded. We didn't speak until the girl left. Now, the washers and dryers were silent, with no empty laundry baskets to be found.

Sarah's long curly hair glistened in the bright lights. Her chestnut eyes smiled. Alone with her finally, I couldn't stop thinking about what it would be like to kiss her for the first time. *Who kisses who, when there's no guy involved?* I'd never made the first move before. And, in college, I'd only kissed guys for the first time when drinking. Stone-cold sober now, how would I do it?

I got up, stretched my legs a bit, then sat back down on the loveseat, just a little bit closer to her than before. I hoped she didn't know I was just pretending I needed to stretch.

I stammered, "Um, you know I am really attracted to you."

A huge grin spread across her face. "I'm attracted to you too."

Our legs rested only a few inches apart. We talked some more, but I didn't really hear her words or know what I was saying. *How can I tell if she wants me to kiss her?* She laughed at something I said and touched my knee for a brief moment, sending a pulse of heat throughout my body.

A skinny guy in a torn black shirt and floppy skater hair walked into the room, causing me to jump. He threw his whites and darks in the same load. It seemed to take him forever to find change and figure out how to use the washer.

The wall clock read 1:30 a.m. Then 2:45. Then 3:15. I pictured kissing her soft lips. *When is the right moment? Will she kiss me back? Will it feel the same as kissing a guy?* 3:30 a.m. 4:15 a.m. I scooted a little closer to her. *Why can't I just get up enough guts to do it already?* Self-doubt filled my head.

The clock on the wall read 5:10 a.m. I said, "So, I have to leave by 5:30, 'cause Jackie and I have to go over to the psych building to wait in line to sign up for Experimental Psychology. The class fills up really fast and if we don't get in this semester, we can't take other classes that have it as a pre-req."

Sarah's face fell. We continued to sit inches from one another, looking into each other's eyes. Neither of us made a move to get off the couch. After a few moments, I said, "Okay, I guess I've gotta go." We very slowly moved off the couch and out of the laundry room.

Alone in the lobby area, we only heard the buzzing of the fluorescent lights overhead. As I arrived at the door, I turned around to face Sarah. I could feel the warmth of her body. I looked around the lobby; nobody else was in sight. We stood motionless, smiling at each other. Nervous energy and excitement propelled me forward.

I quickly leaned in and kissed her on the lips. She kissed back with her soft lips, sweet and delicate. I could barely catch my breath and we pulled away after a few moments. My heart pumped even harder. She smiled at me, sending shots of adrenaline through me. I waved goodbye and opened the door to a cool breeze.

Adrenaline propelled me quickly home, smiling the whole way. I think I might have been skipping just a little. As Jackie and I walked to the psych building, fluorescent pinks and oranges appeared in the sky. Fall leaves crunched under my feet and the damp, earthy smell from the morning dew energized me. The edges of the trees, buildings, and lampposts appeared crisper and more in focus than usual, like when I put my glasses on after waking up in the morning.

21

YOU ARE MY SUNSHINE

November, Junior Year

Knock knock. My heart sped up at the sound. I hurried through my empty living room.

Sarah beamed as I opened the front door to my apartment. After I closed the door, we made out for a few minutes before I said, "You wanna come in and listen to some music?"

We had been talking for hours on the phone almost every night for weeks, about everything from family to classes to roommates to our intense feelings for each other. We saw each other several times a week, stealing kisses whenever we managed to get alone time in her dorm room or mine. I wrote in my journal, "Damn is she a good kisser." These kisses didn't involve alcohol, like most of my hookups with guys had.

The early evening sun was fading fast and only a sliver of light shone through the windows. I closed my bedroom door and popped a CD into the boom box. We lay on my futon mattress, propped against fluffy black and white cow-print pillows that matched the futon cover, wrapping our arms around each other and gazing into each other's eyes. No words were needed. I felt emotionally and physically connected to her in a way I had never experienced before. We started to passionately make out. Lost in the moment, I felt heat build inside me, head to toe.

When we stopped kissing for a brief moment, I noticed the music had ended. We gazed at each other again and suddenly I felt nervous. "I'm going to start the music again." I got up, pressed the "repeat" button on the boom box, then walked over and flipped off the light. Adrenaline rushed through me as I quickly got back on the futon, inches from Sarah. `

She said "Your cologne smells nice" as she nestled in closer, wrapping her arms around me, and moved in for another kiss. Quickly swept away in passion, our hands moved everywhere, all over each other's bodies. Although we were a little shy at first, our desire took over as we undressed. We touched each other in all the right places. It felt powerful, natural, and easy. The intensity overwhelmed me. We lay in each other's arms, kissing off and on for what might have been hours.

I couldn't get enough of this closeness with Sarah and neither could she. Although we were both very busy—her with swim team practice, pre-med classes, and her friends, and me with Theta and my part-time job at the library, we found as much alone time as we could. We quickly decided to be girlfriends—in an exclusive relationship.

One morning when I turned over in bed and opened my eyes, she said "I was watching you sleep, and you looked so peaceful." Then she put her arm around me. After cuddling for a bit, she said she needed to leave for swim practice. After she left, I could still smell her perfume and the scent of her shampoo on the pillow. I breathed it in deeply.

• • •

I told my other two roommates about Sarah, not able to hide it when Sarah came over. They didn't have much of a reaction, positive or negative. It was an awkward conversation, and we never really talked about it after that.

Shortly after Sarah and I became official girlfriends, I asked two of my sorority sisters that I had told about Sarah to help me surprise her. I drove the three of us in my white Volkswagen Fox to Sarah's dorm late one night I knew she would be there.

I said, "So, you'll give Sarah the flower and sing 'You Are My Sunshine'? Cool?"

Chrissy said, "Yes, we'll do it! I can't wait to see her face!" Jackie took the giant yellow sunflower I'd bought at the Schnucks grocery store and got out of the car with Chrissy. I watched them walk toward the entrance of Sarah's dorm, soft light shining out from the door and windows into the dark night. Lampposts lit the pathway.

I sat in the car, tapping my foot on the floor and fidgeting with the stick shift while continuing to stare at the entrance to Sarah's dorm. I waited for what felt like eternity. I finally saw them emerge, no longer holding the sunflower. They talked animatedly to each other, smiling. I intently tried to interpret their body language.

As they opened the car door, I quickly blurted, "So what happened?"

Chrissy said, "So, we went up there and she wasn't in her room. Her roommate was there and told us she was down the hall, so Jackie went to go find her and bring her back."

Jackie chimed in. "Yes, so I found her and told her to come to her room because there was a surprise for her. She looked confused."

Chrissy said, "Yeah, so when Jackie brought her back to her room she looked kind of jumpy, actually. Anyway, I told her that you had gotten the sunflower for her and handed it to her. She was cute and was totally smiling and blushing in front of her roommate. Anyway, so then I told her you had another surprise for her. That's when we started singing to her!"

I said, "So, what did she do?"

Chrissy continued, "She stood there, smiling and blushing, and as we were singing a bunch of people from her dorm came by and started to watch!"

Jackie said, "By the time we finished there were maybe 10 people there! And everyone started asking who the flower was from."

"What did she say?"

Jackie continued, "Well, she didn't really say. She wouldn't tell them."

I could feel my heart sink a little. I was only out to a few people as well, so I understood her reaction. But I had wanted to make her feel special and loved, and it made me sad that it may have made her feel uncomfortable instead.

When I got back to my apartment, Sarah had left a message on my voicemail. I called her back. She said it was the sweetest thing anyone had ever done for her, even though she felt a little embarrassed from all the attention and didn't know what to say when everyone asked whom it was from. She said some of the other girls seemed really jealous and said they couldn't imagine a guy doing anything that romantic—he must be a major catch! We laughed as we reveled in our secret.

22

JAILBREAK

November, Junior Year

Sarah and I wove through the densely packed crowd in the massive basement. KAPPA ALPHA THETA JAILBREAK '93 was painted on a sign on the concrete wall, in black with yellow handcuffs. A floor-to-ceiling chain-link fence enclosed the dance floor on all four sides, a few hundred people packed into the claustrophobic space.

We jostled past sweaty bodies into the packed dance area. The fog machine spit out a cloud of smoke and the disco ball reflected in the hazy air, which smelled of cigarette smoke, sour beer, sweat, and dry ice.

Because of the lack of space, we all danced closely together. Straight couples were grinding up against each other, arms and legs intertwined. Some kissed. I looked on, remembering previous sorority and frat parties when that had been me.

Daniela and I danced and jumped and smiled to "You Shook Me All Night Long" by AC/DC, along with many of my sisters. I danced as far from Sarah as possible, with only brief moments of eye contact. I had a hard time containing my smile as Sarah smiled at me. I imagined what it would feel like to press my body against hers, wrapping my arms around her; to have her arms wrapped around me, chest to chest, making out. *If we dance closer, will people be able to tell we're together? If we make too much eye contact, will others see our looks for what they really are?*

Officially girlfriends, in an exclusive relationship, we had spent many nights together having sex and talking for hours. Here, we acted like not much more than strangers. Of the few hundred people at the party, only Daniela and Simon, my two roommates, and a sister that sang "You Are My Sunshine" knew Sarah and I were together. I kept an eye out for stares and questioning looks from others, but couldn't detect any. I remembered back to sorority parties in the past and how I used to dance with my sisters with abandon. Now I felt distracted and inhibited. Every moment, I fought my compulsion for closeness with Sarah. Her presence pulled me in, but I fought against it.

Constant thoughts swirled through my head. *Sarah looks so beautiful. I really wish I could dance with her.* Fast song after fast song played, the crowd dancing wildly to the music. *What would happen if we were to dance together?* I'd never seen a gay couple dance together before, on campus or anywhere. I'd never seen gay people hold hands or show any PDA anywhere, even in an all-gay setting like GLBA. I didn't know of any gay people in any sorority or fraternity. *Would people stare?*

Sarah smiled at me and I looked away. She moved closer and I spun to face away from her.

Then, a slow song came on: Peter Gabriel's "In Your Eyes." My stomach clenched into a knot. Daniela and Simon began to dance, arms around each other, Daniela's head resting on Simon's shoulder. Dozens of other straight couples joined together, embracing and swaying slowly to the music. I stood frozen, unable to move. I looked into Sarah's hopeful eyes as she stood motionless, as if waiting for me. I imagined her arms around mine, moving cheek to cheek.

I leaned in, but was careful not to touch her. "Hey, can we take a break?"

Her shoulders sank. "I guess so."

The words to the love song played and burned into my head.

I quickly pushed out of the fenced-in "jail." Sarah followed me up the concrete stairs. Opening the door, I felt a slap of cold air against my face. We stood alone, not touching, in the grassy area in front of the dorm.

Tears threatened to break loose. "I'm sorry I couldn't dance with you. I really wanted to. I just couldn't."

She said, "I know. I wanted to dance with you too. It's hard."

I stuck my hands in my jacket pockets. I shook my head and said, "Sarah, I'm so sorry. I love you so much."

She continued to listen, not making a sound.

"And I do wanna tell all my sisters about you. I'm just…I'm just really afraid. I'm just scared. I'm so sorry."

Sarah said, "I know. I'm sorry too." We didn't go back to the Jailbreak party.

A few days later, some sisters greeted me with hugs in the Theta suite. We sat at the table with our lunches. My spicy black bean chili steamed in its Styrofoam bowl.

Helena looked at the huge framed composite picture with photos of all 100+ women in our sorority hanging on the wall. In the rows of circular headshot photos, everyone wore identical black draping over their shoulders, tilted their head in the exact same deferential way, and had long, styled hair and makeup. Our photo shoot look was mandated by the sorority and reinforced by the photographer. The effect was of complete uniformity—any individual self-expression stripped away before we got in front of the camera. Pictures identical to this appeared in every sorority suite, all the same except for the small sorority letters at the top.

The message was loud and clear: don't show anything that makes you seem too different. This message caused me such an internal struggle. Not just my sexual orientation, but my gender identity too stood in sharp contrast to my sisters'.

Helena enthusiastically said, "Let's try to guess who is a virgin and who isn't. It'll be fun! I'll go first. I'm not a virgin!"

Everyone smiled.

Helena looked around at the rest of us, one by one. After a few moments of silence, I said, "Okay, I'm not a virgin either."

Helena said, "That's no surprise!"

"Ha ha," I said jokingly. *Little do they know I can count the number of times I've had traditional hetero sex on two hands.*

Tegan, Rachel, and Shannon remained quiet. Helena and I looked at them expectantly. The only noise was the soft humming of the refrigerator in the small kitchenette.

Rachel finally said, "Okay, I'm no longer a virgin either. My boyfriend and I finally did it!"

I thought about Rachel's charismatic boyfriend, a member of one of the most popular fraternities. Rachel always beamed as he swung her around on the dance floor during our sorority parties.

Helena said "Finally!"

We all turned our attention to Tegan and Shannon.

Bashfully Shannon said, "No. I'm still a virgin. I guess I just haven't found the right guy."

"Okay, Tegan, what about you?" Helena asked.

After a moment of hesitation, Tegan said, "I'm still a virgin."

"Really?" Helena asked.

"Yeah, we're waiting. We're both kind of traditional like that." I had met Tegan's cute, soft-spoken engineering major boyfriend a few times at parties.

As the discussion progressed, I started to squirm. Anxious energy churned in my stomach and thoughts swirled through my head. *What if one of them asks me about my love life? What am I going to say? I know they're going to. Should I make an excuse and leave now?*

Too late. I heard Helena say, "So what's the scoop with you, Kristin?"

After a moment of silence, I looked up and saw all four of them staring at me expectedly. "What?"

Helena smiled and said, "Who are you dating? I know you must have something going on. You always do!"

I maintained a death grip on the sides of my padded chair. I wanted to say, "Guys, I've got a girlfriend now! Her name is Sarah. She's beautiful and sweet and smart and caring. She's pre-med and a freshman and on the swim team. Our kisses are unbelievable and the sex is so hot! I've never felt this way before about anyone. We're so in love and I can't wait for you to meet her!"

Instead, I sat silent for a few moments, running various scenarios through my head. If I said everything I was thinking but replaced

Sarah's name with "Todd" and changed a few pronouns, I knew I would hear "Oh my God! That's awesome! I'm so happy for you. He sounds amazing! I can't wait to meet him!" Squeals of excitement would fill the room with smiles and questions from everyone.

Then I began to imagine what would happen if I told them about Sarah. I imagined dead silence all around the table and frowns staring back at me. Helena would ask "What? What did you say?" I would repeat myself and everyone would avoid eye contact. An uncomfortable silence would start.

Then Shannon would say "Hmm. That's interesting" with a frown on her face. Tegan would be squirming the most because she would be thinking I was going to Hell. Then Helena would say, "Hey guys, I've got to finish up some homework, so I better get going." Everyone else would chime in, "Uh, yeah. Me too." On the way out, my sisters would skip out without hugging me or if they did it would just be a quick, limp hug.

I heard Helena say, "So? What's the scoop? Details!!"

Her voice jolted me back into the present. Avoiding eye contact, I said, "I'm not really dating anyone."

A few days ago, I had written in my journal, "I want to feel comfortable in the chapter and like I can be me. I feel like I have this big secret and like I will burst soon unless I quit hiding it." As the minutes dragged on and I stared at the sorority composite picture, I knew I couldn't do it. I didn't have the strength to risk the outcomes I feared.

Tegan said, "That's so unlike you. You're not hanging out with anyone? Jake? No fun hookup stories?"

I fidgeted in my seat as I ran through options of what to say. Finally, I managed to blurt out "Yeah, Jake and I still hang out sometimes." I felt sick inside for lying, for not having the courage to be truthful. For disrespecting my relationship with Sarah. For being ashamed to be gay.

I felt like an outsider, disconnected. To them, nothing had changed. But for me, everything had changed. I held a secret that I didn't want to keep, but felt I had to. I left the suite feeling dejected, lonely, and supremely conflicted.

23

IN YOUR EYES

November, Junior Year

I downed a couple shots, a screwdriver, and two beers before we left. The alcohol warmed my chest, and I hoped it would give me the courage I needed tonight, or at least make it so I didn't care what others thought. My stomach clenched, making me hunch over in pain.

The week before, I had visited campus medical services because my stomach had been in almost constant pain. It felt a bit like getting kicked in the stomach by a soccer ball, knocking the wind out of me. I'd had the pains in my stomach since sophomore year, but it had been much worse over the past couple of months. My psychologist thought it was because I was stressed out; I knew she was right.

As I thought about going on the dance floor with Sarah, I felt another punch in my gut. Fleeing the Jailbreak party when "In Your Eyes" came on a couple of months ago still tormented me. *Why am I such a coward?* I could barely stand up straight as Sarah, Daniela, Simon, some of my sorority sisters and their dates, and I walked briskly to our sorority "pajama party" in the quad, lamps lighting our path across campus.

On our way I thought about my past experiences in the quad, a square of regal-looking buildings surrounding a grassy area. It was most fondly known for the annual WILD event in the spring. Freshman year, I had joined some of my sorority sisters there. We arrived shortly after lunch to couches, BBQ grills, and kegs of cheap beer—like a football tailgate party, but instead of a game, rock bands are the main event. We stopped by an area filled with Kappa Sigma guys, who served us foamy beer in plastic cups and grilled hot dogs and hamburgers. We munched on our food and chatted with the guys, tall trees providing some shade.

After several beers at WILD, Mackenzie, a Theta in my pledge class, and I had to pee. After arriving at the bathroom, we saw the line was long. We waited for a few moments, then decided to squat in the bushes instead, laughing uncontrollably, the bright sunshine shining down on us.

Because of the massive amounts of hookups, due to the large amount of alcohol consumed, WILD was commonly called "walk-in get laid." We heard stories about people having sex in the bushes or on the roof of the library. At my first WILD freshman year, I was wasted before the bands came on at dusk, so I missed them.

During WILD my sophomore year, I was drinking with some of my sisters when I spotted a guy with a University of Texas baseball cap. The white longhorn on the burnt orange hat caught my eye as he and some buddies tossed a football. My mom worked at the University of Texas in Austin, so I recognized the logo.

"I like your hat," I yelled.

My memory is a bit vague about what transpired between "I like your hat" at 4 p.m. and his on-campus apartment after dark. The next thing I remember is lying naked on his single mattress on the floor, him struggling to tear open a condom and pull it on his hard dick.

"I'm not going to have sex with you," I said. He kneeled above me and I unpeeled his condom and threw it on the floor.

"Oh, come on," he said in a lighthearted manner. He proceeded to grab another condom out of the top drawer of his bedside table, rip it open, and place it on his still-hard dick.

"No," I declared and again removed the condom, tossing it on the floor. This process repeated itself a few more times until it was almost comical. He finally gave up and we didn't have sex. He got dressed and left the bedroom while I got dressed.

The rug was covered with crumpled clothes and six condoms. I opened the door to his bedroom and turned right toward the living room. As I walked in, he was sitting on the couch with two other guys—and two girls from my pledge class, Chrissy and Tegan. I felt my face flushing hot. I had no idea anyone else was there.

Chrissy grabbed my hand and said to the others, "We'll be back." She led me into the guy's bedroom. Looking at all the condoms lying on the floor she exclaimed, "Kristin!" with a sly smile on her face.

I said, "No, seriously, it's not what you think. He kept putting condoms on and I kept taking them off because I didn't want to have sex with him!"

Chrissy smiled at me mischievously, stared at the condoms on the floor, then back at me, and started to laugh loudly. Then I started to laugh too. Later that evening, the guy walked me to my dorm room and gave me his phone number. I don't remember his name. I never called him.

A year later, I knew tonight's excursion to the quad was going to be completely different. Walking into one of the majestic buildings surrounding the quad brought me into another world. The cavernous hall with rich wood floors and paneling made me feel like I was at Harvard, or what I thought Harvard would look like. The conservative space seemed like an odd place for tonight's pajama-themed party. Guys with plaid flannel pants, blue boxers, and white T-shirts moved stiffly to the music. Girls wore lacy nightgowns, silky lingerie, or cotton sleep pants. Sarah and I both wore cotton pajama pants and long-sleeve shirts. The room felt cold and impersonal and Sarah and I kept our distance while "Groove Is in the Heart" by Deee-Lite played. It was a completely different feeling than the Jailbreak party, where we were all packed in an extremely small space with low ceilings, sweating together. Now it was winter and chilly inside.

Depeche Mode, New Order, and the Eurythmics blasted over the speakers. The DJ had great taste in music. That's because most of it was actually mine. I looked behind the DJ table at Jake in the Hat. He always DJed at the Kappa Sigma parties and I had recommended him for our party. He had come over and borrowed most of my 100 or so CDs, like he always did before parties. I knew which ones he borrowed because when he returned them, they had a little piece of cut notebook paper inside that said "Kristin" written in neat letters. His white blond hair bobbed to the beat behind the DJ table.

The party was scheduled to end at 2 a.m. and it was already 1 a.m. During slow songs, Sarah and I sat on the chairs lining the walls, watching the other couples dancing—like the girls who sat waiting for a boy to ask them to dance in junior high. I constantly felt my hand drawn to hers, wanting to hold it, and I had to keep reminding myself not to, even as we watched all the straight couples holding hands and kissing.

Not only had I never seen any same-sex couple kissing or holding hands anywhere on campus, I had never heard of anyone doing it either. Not only had I never seen two women slow dance together at a sorority function, I had never heard of two women doing it anywhere, ever. Any same-sex PDA felt like a monumental act of defiance, not only of norms on campus, but especially against the homogenous straight culture of my sorority and the Greek system in general.

I imagined Sarah and me locked in an embrace on the dance floor with everyone else. I hated sitting on the sidelines. "You're such a coward" looped on repeat in my mind.

We sat in silence, looking in from the outside. I looked longingly at the couples slow dancing. The crowd had thinned out to about 50 people. Time was running out for me. I clenched my fists as if bracing for battle and turned to Sarah and said, "I'll be right back."

I walked toward Jake in the Hat. "Hey," I said, trying to act casual.

He replied, "Hey. What's up?"

I looked at him, then out at the crowd, then turned back to him. "I have a request."

"Okay, what do you want?"

"Can you play 'In Your Eyes' by Peter Gabriel?" Alone in my room, I'd listened to the song countless times since the Jailbreak night. I replayed it dozens of times, asking myself why I didn't have more courage.

"Sure," he said.

I walked back. Sarah's eyebrows raised in what seemed to be a question. I smiled at her and she smiled back as we danced to the

Pet Shop Boys "So Hard", still making sure to keep our distance. I couldn't stop myself from smiling when I was around Sarah. I thought about the night before in my room. We'd spent hours having hot, sweaty sex, and our kisses and cuddling lasted for hours after that.

I was abruptly taken out of my fantasy world as "In Your Eyes" began to play. Simon and Daniela immediately joined together, as did the 25 or so couples left. Sarah started toward the chairs at the perimeter of the hall.

I blurted, "Do you wanna dance?"

Looking surprised, she stopped. "Really?"

"Yes."

I took a deep breath and felt another strong punch in the gut. We hesitantly moved toward each other. I looked around to see if anyone was watching us. Everyone seemed occupied with each other. We stopped close, face to face. She didn't move and neither did I. Then I slowly placed my right hand on her left hip and my left hand on her right hip. Our eyes locked. She reached her arms toward my neck and asked, "Is this okay?"

I stammered "Yes." Even as my stomach clenched harder, her touch sent warm shivers of pleasure down my body. Her arms circled my neck and she pulled in closer until our bodies touched. She rested her head on my left shoulder, nuzzling into my neck. I could feel her long hair brush against my skin.

My eyes remained wide open as one by one, the stares started. I felt my face burn. Some people looked confused. Some looked angry. Some looked disgusted. I could see couples whisper to each other as they looked at us. Some pointed at us or stopped moving altogether. I couldn't see Sarah's face, since her head was nuzzled into my neck.

I didn't even hear the music. Frowns hit me from all directions as I tried not to make eye contact with anyone. I tried to focus on Sarah and enjoy the moment, but I couldn't—all I felt was the stares.

The song felt like it lasted forever. When it finally ended, I avoided eye contact with everyone except Sarah. I didn't look around the hall or even at Daniela.

I quickly said to Sarah, "You ready to go?"

"Uh, sure."

As we escaped out the door, the searing wind slapped me in the face. I took out a Marlboro Red, lit it, inhaled deeply, and felt the bitter smoke in my lungs. We walked back in silence as I smoked two more cigarettes in quick succession. Sarah looked at me with sympathetic eyes as I took another drag.

Walking quickly, I was overcome with thoughts hurtling through my head. *How will I face everyone in my sorority? Will everyone be talking behind my back? Will I get kicked out of my sorority?*

Somehow, I had expected to enjoy dancing close with Sarah. I had held out hope that my worries were all in my head, that everyone would be fine with it and that I was making a big deal out of nothing. The grimaces, stares, and whispers told me I was wrong. I had fantasized that I would somehow feel more complete and accepted while dancing with Sarah and surrounded by friends. Instead I felt lonelier than ever.

24

SPRING BREAK

March, Junior Year

Sarah and I sat in the back seat holding hands while Simon drove us on a two-lane road in the dark toward our destination of South Padre Island, located on the southeastern tip of Texas off the Gulf of Mexico. After driving 18 hours from St. Louis, we planned to spend our spring break in one of the hottest party destinations in the U.S.

We arrived at our cheap motel very late that night. Our room held a queen-size bed and a couch that folded into a bed. Sarah and I climbed into the fold-out bed. I could feel the springs underneath my back.

When we heard Simon start to snore and no longer heard any movement or sound from Daniela, Sarah whispered, "Can you be quiet?"

I whispered, "Yes."

Afterward, we lay face-to-face, embracing one another, breathing hard.

She softly said, "I love you."

I whispered back, "I love you too."

We squeezed in closer and kissed. The only sound in the room came from Simon's intermittent snoring. We both fell quickly asleep.

• • •

In the morning, we awoke to dark clouds, rain, and cool temperatures. In the lobby the weather forecast was posted as "cloudy with a good chance of rain" the entire week of our spring break. Too cold even for shorts. Disappointment spread across our faces as we looked at the forecast, then at each other.

One night, the four of us plus some of Simon's frat brothers met up at a bar in Mexico, just across the border. At the entrance, scantily clad Mexican women greeted us holding trays of clear plastic cups.

One woman said in a heavy accent, "Tip your head back and open your mouth." I did as she said, and she poured the liquid into my mouth. The tequila burned my throat, and some of it trickled out onto my T-shirt. I watched as Daniela, Simon, and Sarah gulped their shots as well.

Inside the packed bar sat two dentist chairs on either side of the entry, just inside the doors. A line formed around each chair. We watched as another young Mexican woman spun the person in the chair around, then abruptly stopped the chair and poured tequila from a large bottle into his mouth, while pouring a bottle of sour mix simultaneously into his mouth with the other hand. The guy shook his head back and forth to slosh the liquid around, then swallowed with a big gulp, and the crowd erupted in cheers. The next person took his place in the dentist's chair.

We got in line and paid $1 each for an upside-down margarita. The dive bar was hot, humid, and loud, packed with hundreds of college students on spring break. When it was my turn, the young woman placed a small towel over my chest. In heavily accented

English, she said, "Put your head back." I tilted my head back and she quickly poured tequila, then margarita mix in my mouth. As I tried closing my mouth, the sticky liquid overflowed and dribbled down my neck and chest. I swallowed, the tangy liquid burning my throat. Then she spun me around and around in the chair. When the chair stopped, I tried to get up, but wobbled. I grabbed the side of the chair and waited until my head cleared before I let go, walked unsteadily a few feet, then waited for Sarah, Daniela, and Simon.

We grabbed Coronas with a slice of lime for $2 each. Then we hit the tiny dance floor, filled primarily with college students. Top 40 music blasted from the speakers and we danced vigorously to the pounding beats.

A guy with a baseball cap spotted Sarah and moved toward her from behind. About two feet away from me, I saw him press up against her back, put his hand on her hip, and start gyrating behind her. Sarah looked surprised, then her brows furrowed.

I pictured pushing him away, telling him she was my girlfriend, and pulling her toward me to dance. Instead I fumed inside and turned to face Simon and Daniela, so I didn't have to watch. It felt like fire was shooting from my ears. I looked back over my shoulder at Sarah. The guy was still slobbering all over her, towering above her. Luckily, he stumbled off after a few minutes. My heart was still racing from having to watch him dancing with Sarah. After a couple more songs, she came closer and yelled "Is everything okay?"

I shouted back, "Not exactly."

She touched my arm and said, "What's wrong?"

I folded my arms. "I couldn't stand seeing that guy dancing with you."

"I know. I was trying to give him signals I wasn't into it, but he wasn't getting it." She squeezed my arm.

She brushed my arm quickly with her hand, then we looked around. Nobody seemed to be watching us. I backed away a little and we started dancing again.

• • •

The four of us went out dancing every night and the same thing happened. I spent a lot of time imagining dancing with Sarah, our bodies pressed together, moving to the quick pulsing music—but only in my imagination. There were no gay couples dancing together. The reality was that drunk guys kept trying to dance with both Sarah and me, assuming we were single. We both spent a lot of time trying to escape them. I imagined yelling, "Get off my girlfriend!"

Nights on the dance floor brought up memories of slow dancing with Sarah at the pajama party. While I was proud that I'd had the courage to dance with Sarah, I still cringed at how uncomfortable the stares and frowns felt. The fact that none of my sisters ever mentioned the dance or asked about Sarah after that communicated their lack of interest or discomfort at best, disapproval at worst. If I had danced with a guy they hadn't seen me with before, my sisters would have squealed with excitement as they asked for every minute detail of how we had met and what he was like. I often felt on edge around them, like my true self wasn't good enough, and I started to disengage.

One of the nights when Sarah was wasted—a very rare occasion— she said she was worried I might think she had no personality and was boring. I assured her I didn't feel that way at all. Her personality was much more mellow than mine; she was less expressive and less adventurous, but after about four months of dating, I absolutely didn't think her personality was boring.

It rained all week except for the second-to-last day we were there. Clouds floated across the gray sky, but at least it wasn't raining. We all put on our bathing suits. I lathered SPF 15 on Sarah's pale skin, and she returned the favor. When we arrived, the beach was packed with thousands of bathing suit–clad students holding Coronas at various makeshift parties. Loudspeakers, stages, buckets of cold beer, and hot men and women handed out drinks. As we walked, the cool sand squished beneath my feet.

That night Sarah and I looked like cooked lobsters. Our skin glowed bright pink, except where our bathing suits covered it. I rubbed aloe vera gel on her bare back, shoulders, chest, and legs, and got her a loose shirt to wear. Carefully, she then spread the cool gel on my hot skin. The air blowing from the fan onto my skin made me shiver. Afterward, we sat on the bed, held hands, and turned on the TV.

The next day the four of us drove back to St. Louis. Our one week of paradise came to an end and I wasn't quite ready for my busy routine of classes, studying in the library, running psychology experiments, and Sunday-evening sorority chapter meetings and events. Once we got back to our busy schedules, Sarah and I were only able to see each other a couple times a week and to talk on the phone occasionally. Finding time with Sarah while she managed her busy schedule of classes, studying, swim team practice, her friends, and practice for the musical *Hair* proved challenging.

I often found myself at GLBA meetings and then going to Fallout, the local gay dance club, with my new GLBA friends. Sarah was too busy to join. At the meetings I met Valentina, a spicy Latina lesbian, who had already graduated college and worked at the medical school. She often came out dancing with us and always started dirty dancing with me, putting her hands on my hips from behind and pulling me close, her chest against my back. I felt a twinge of guilt, but not enough to pull away.

Being able to dance freely with a woman was a novelty that felt exhilarating. Despite being in love with Sarah, I developed a crush on Valentina during those nights with her on the dance floor. Her spontaneity, passionate personality, and beauty drew me in. During this time when Sarah and I were busy and not able to see each other much, I asked that our relationship not be exclusive. Sarah reluctantly agreed. Secretly I hoped that Valentina might be interested in me.

25

MARDI GRAS

May, Junior Year

At our weekly Sunday-night sorority chapter meeting, our social chair announced that our formal this year would be Mardi Gras–themed and held in a very swanky hotel downtown. "I'll post the sign-up sheet in our suite tonight. Just add your name and your date's name. I guarantee he'll have a night to remember!" Everyone cheered.

I heard the word "he" loud and clear. Could I even bring a woman to formal? I had never heard of anyone doing that. I had invited Sarah to two of our sorority parties, but they were not formal events and people often brought friends. This was different.

Still, nobody from my sorority had explicitly said anything to me about slow dancing with Sarah at the pajama party. Only my roommates and two sisters knew Sarah and I were dating for sure, because we had talked about it. I didn't know if others in my sorority knew I was gay because they saw me dancing with Sarah, or what they assumed. It reminded me of a WASP-y passive aggressive family that never talks about anything substantial and avoids conflict at all costs—until someone finally explodes from all the repressed feelings. I felt like everyone was in avoidance mode and an explosion could happen at any moment.

A couple of weeks later, I found myself in the sorority suite for the third time since the formal sign-up sheet had been posted. I had asked Sarah to come with me and she'd responded with a resounding "Yes!"

I thought to myself, *I wish Sarah's name was ambiguous, like Pat, like the androgynous character on Saturday Night Live.*

In the sorority suite, groups of girls gathered around the list, writing names on it and gossiping. The list stretched a few pages long.

If I write Sarah's name, what will my sisters say behind my back? "Kristin is going with a girl? She couldn't find a guy to go with her?" "Is she even allowed to bring a girl? Isn't that against the rules?" "I don't want some lesbian in our sorority. Then people won't want to join Theta or will think we are all dykes." "I'm going to be seriously embarrassed in front of my date if some lesbian thing is going on."

I made some small talk with some of my sisters until I saw that nobody was standing near the list. I walked over to it and pulled a pen out of my backpack, my hand shaking. I took the top off my pen and scanned the room again. Everyone looked occupied. I turned back to the sign-up sheet. Quickly, I wrote my name and Sarah's name, at the bottom of the list on the third page. I printed in messy block letters, like I always did—more like most guys' writing, unlike the bubbly cursive of the other names. People often joked that I should be a doctor because of my handwriting. I quickly shoved the cap on the pen and scurried out of the suite.

When I looked at my watch, I saw that I would need to go directly to the psych building to run one of my experiments. I had scored an independent study as a research assistant for my professor from Abnormal Psychology. Once inside the building, I unlocked the lab, grabbed the tape recorder and equipment, and hurried to the experiment room. I set up the equipment, then pulled my script out of my backpack.

A student knocked. I told her to sit in the chair across from me, then explained what to expect. I closed the door, then pressed "play" on the tape recorder. A recording of me calmly and slowly reading a script to hypnotize the subject started. My voice on the recorder instructed the student to close her eyes. Once the tape ended, I asked the student to complete different tasks that measured whether she was hypnotized.

I told her there was a fly buzzing by her ear (there wasn't). She swatted at it. I told her to open her eyes and showed her three plastic blocks. I told her there were two blocks and asked her how many there were; she said "two." I told her I was going to put some vinegar under her nose and for her to sniff it; she scrunched up her nose in disgust as if smelling vinegar (it was water). She was undeniably hypnotized. Then, I had her draw something and timed her. After the experiment was over, I brought her out of hypnosis. When she opened her eyes again, she looked a little confused, which was typical. I thanked her for her time and gave her some cash. Then I packed up and wrote up the results.

On my way back to my dorm, I thought about how I didn't believe hypnosis was possible until I started to work on the experiments and saw people actually get hypnotized. I had to see it for myself to believe it. According to my professor, people who are more artistic are more likely to be able to be hypnotized, but people who are more scientific and less in touch with their emotional and creative sides can't be. I asked another research assistant to try to hypnotize me once. By this time I had spent a lot of energy trying to avoid my true emotions, so I wasn't surprised that it didn't work.

As I walked past blooming tulips and trees beginning to sprout small green buds, I imagined what it would feel like to dance with Sarah at the Theta formal. I pictured how beautiful she would look all dressed up, and smiled to myself.

As Sarah, Daniela, Simon, and I had a drink in our hotel room, thoughts swirled in my head. *How are people going to react when Sarah and I walk into the formal together?* Nobody had said anything to me after I wrote Sarah's name on the sign-up sheet, or after we slow-danced at the pajama party. *Did anyone realize I was bringing a woman, other than a few of my sisters that I was close with? If they did notice, did they just assume Sarah and I were friends? Or were they saying nasty things behind my back?* I felt like I was in a soundproof room where I could see people talking animatedly outside but I couldn't hear them and didn't know what they were saying. Most of my sisters' body language told me they felt uncomfortable and awkward, but was that just in my head? The uncertainty was driving me nuts.

Finishing off a Corona, Daniela said, "You guys ready to go down?"

Simon said, "Yeah, let's go."

I paused but managed to utter, "Um, sure."

I looked at Sarah and smiled weakly. She smiled back and said, "Yeah, I'm ready."

My dress wasn't technically a dress, although it looked like one. It had spaghetti straps, was low-cut and fitted on top, and the bottom swished with floor-length loose pants. Large white polka dots covered the black crepe-like material. The jumpsuit wasn't mine—I had borrowed it from one of my sorority sisters. I had gotten rid of the one dress I owned and had no desire to buy another one. I had never seen any of my sisters not wear a dress at formal, but couldn't stomach wearing a dress again. Dresses always made me feel like I was pretending to be someone that I wasn't. I never understood the excitement my sisters seemed to feel about putting on gowns, heels, elaborate makeup, and styling their hair for hours. Throughout my life I had fought against wearing dresses and skirts and had only done it when the uneasiness from wearing a dress was more than the discomfort I knew I would feel from looking different.

Sarah had pinned a corsage with white and purple flowers onto the strap of my jumpsuit. She wore a white tuxedo shirt, black bowtie, a deep purple vest, black jacket, a short tight black skirt, and black heels. Her long curly brown hair bounced on her shoulders.

The four of us left the hotel room and stepped into the hallway. Anxiety consumed me as I knew I might really be coming out tonight. If people thought Sarah and I might have just been friends at the pajama party, they wouldn't think that after tonight. I had never heard of anyone bringing someone of the same sex to any sorority or fraternity formal, and knew I might be the first. Stepping into the hallway, I wasn't sure whether my fear or the emotional pain of not standing up for myself was worse. I would soon find out.

Simon took Daniela's hand. I took a deep breath and, as I took Sarah's hand, fear, strength, joy, and anxiety coursed through me. She squeezed my hand and smiled at me encouragingly. Both of us struggled to be completely out to all our friends, so we commiserated about how scary it could be. I felt like we were in it together. We walked down the long corridor toward the elevator. It was empty. I breathed a sigh of relief. This was the first time we had held hands in a public setting.

As we waited for the elevator, Daniela and Simon were lost in their own world, gazing adoringly at each other. The doors slowly opened to reveal two guys in tuxes, talking loudly. As we got on, I felt the guys staring at Sarah and me, but avoided eye contact with them. Out of the corner of my eye I saw one guy nudge the other one with his elbow and say "Check it out," nodding his head toward us and looking at our hands.

The other guy looked at our hands joined together, then at us. Chuckling, he said, "Yeah, girls. That's, uh, hot."

The other guy laughed, swaying slightly. He then said, "Yeah, man, that's cool." His slimy smile oozed toward us.

Our hands parted as we exited the elevator and entered the expansive grand ballroom. Shimmering chandeliers hung from the ceilings. Tables covered with Mardi Gras beads and bouquets of yellow and red flowers brightened the atmosphere.

Clean-cut guys wearing classic black and white tuxes filled the ballroom. A few men wearing regular suits and ties were interspersed in the line to the bar. All my sorority sisters wore high heels, shiny jewelry, and formal dresses, with coiffed hair, manicured nails, and lots of makeup.

As we entered, the hired photographer snapped a picture of the four of us with his huge camera. My friend Chrissy, who was one of my few sisters that knew Sarah and I were together, immediately saw us and walked our way. She gave all four of us hugs.

She looked at Sarah and I and said, "You guys look cute together!"

I blushed and bashfully said thanks. Nobody had ever said this to Sarah and me. Although it felt amazing to have our relationship recognized in this way, it had been such a long time coming.

On the dance floor, most guys were doing that awkward white boy shuffle. They stiffly swayed back and forth with a look of "I know I look like an idiot and I'd rather be getting wasted at the bar or watching football. I hope this song ends soon." Although the majority of guys fell into this camp, there were five or six guys that thought they were God's gift to dancing, trying to do some sort of hip-hop moves with their legs and arms flailing about, while their dates looked on in horror and danced as far away from them as possible. They were funny to watch. I was just glad they weren't my date!

Chrissy's comment about us looking cute together put a spring in my step. I thought to myself, *maybe things won't be as awkward as I think.* By now, all three of my roommates, plus three of my sorority sisters knew about Sarah, one of whom was my pledge mom.

On our way to the buffet table we ran in to Adrienne, my pledge mom. She hugged Daniela and me. We never ended up being as close as I was to sisters in my pledge class or spending a lot of time together, but she was someone I enjoyed being around. She always exuded positive energy and a genuineness that put me at ease.

I said to Adrienne, "This is my girlfriend, Sarah."

Adrienne exuded warmth and hugged Sarah, saying, "So nice to meet you."

Sarah smiled and said, "Nice to meet you too."

Adrienne's comment gave me another infusion of positive energy. As Simon left to get us all beers from the bar, Daniela, Sarah, and I helped ourselves to shrimp cocktail, pasta, and chicken. We sat at one of the half-empty tables.

At the table, I whispered to Sarah, "How are you doing? Are you feeling okay?"

"I'm okay. I'm worried, but it will be okay." She squeezed my hand underneath the table and smiled. She then said, "You look pretty."

I smiled back and said, "So do you."

"Tainted Love" by Soft Cell started playing and the four of us moved onto the packed dance floor. I scanned the crowd, and everyone looked lost in their own worlds, dancing to the music. Many straight couples were grinding on each other, free from inhibition. Some couples made out. The four of us danced in a little circle, Sarah and I maintaining eye contact, dancing closely but not yet touching. At least I didn't have to worry about guys trying to dirty dance with Sarah, and I felt more relaxed, despite anxiety about fully coming out.

A few of my other sisters and their dates joined us. A bunch of us swayed to the beat in a big circle.

Megan grabbed me by the arm, smiling, and said "She's cute!"

I said back "I know!"

A slow song came on—"Lady in Red." Other couples' bodies joined together. I stood staring at Sarah, and she stared back with a questioning look. This was the first sorority event Sarah had been to with me since the pajama party.

After a few moments, Sarah stepped closer to me. I glanced around us, looking at all the couples locked in an embrace, then slowly stepped toward her. I held up my hand. She took it and I pulled her in. She wrapped her arms around my neck and I pulled her in at the waist until I could feel her against my chest. She held me tight.

She whispered "I love you" in my ear.

I whispered back, "I love you too." I could feel her breath on my neck. Our bodies moved ever so slightly to the music as I pulled her in tighter.

Suddenly, I heard a deep voice say, "Can you turn and face the camera?"

We both turned toward the voice. A tall cameraman held a long lens pointed directly at us. He said "Smile!" and reflexively we both smiled, and he snapped the picture. His sly smile lingered on us, then he turned and walked away.

Sarah and I looked at each other, shrugging our shoulders. I scanned the crowd again and noticed a few people staring at us, frowning—some of my sisters, some of their dates. Some wore looks of confusion, others looks of disgust. Some frowned, but a few smiled.

"Lady in Red" ended and another slow song started to play. I looked at Sarah, checking in, and we continued dancing, as did most of the other couples. I turned my head slightly toward her cheek and kissed it. She moved so we were face to face, our noses almost touching, and we leaned in ever so slightly and kissed. As we gazed into each other's eyes we again heard "Smile!"

We turned and the photographer stood a few feet away with his massive black and silver metal camera. He snapped another picture.

Later, when Sarah and I wandered over to the buffet and started putting fruit on a plate, the photographer materialized out of nowhere again. "Why don't you feed her a piece of fruit for the camera?"

Sarah and I just looked at each other, communicating "What is with this guy?" with our eyes. She shrugged her shoulders and I picked up a spherical piece of green honeydew melon and moved it toward Sarah's mouth. I heard a *click* as Sarah opened her mouth and I popped it in. We laughed.

Sarah said, "That guy is totally following us around."

"I don't know whether it's creepy or funny."

"A little of both."

He was on us for the rest of the night—we couldn't get rid of him. At all the sorority parties I had been to previously, I always felt like I had to hunt down the photographer, so I could get at least one or two pictures by the end of the night. But this guy must've snapped 20 pictures of us. Every few minutes he would seemingly materialize out of nowhere, magically appearing in front of us like he was teleported. Then, *click.*

On the way back to the dance floor, Jade, a sister in my pledge class, walked directly toward us. She stared at me, then at Sarah, then back at me with daggers—and then changed course and walked far around us, avoiding us. My shoulders sunk as I watched her walk away quickly.

Immediately after, Jan, another sister from my pledge class, was dancing as we approached. She looked at us then weakly said "Hey," frowning at Sarah. She gave me a limp hug, like the awkward pat that straight guys give each other, then let go quickly and took off before I could introduce Sarah or say anything.

Sarah said, "She seemed kind of rude."

"Yeah, she did." I felt tears welling up in my eyes at the rejection from someone I thought was my friend.

Then the photographer appeared out of thin air right in front of us again. "Say cheese!" We looked up reflexively. *Click.*

Another slow song came on. Sarah asked if I was okay.

"I guess. It just hurts that some people I thought were my friends are acting distant and cold."

I wondered what things would be like after this. After tonight, there would be no mistaking that I had a girlfriend. *Who's going to still be friends with me?* What made me the most uncomfortable was that none of my sisters said anything overtly negative to my face or addressed it directly; I could just feel their disapproval and awkwardness, tainting our interactions. Some of my sisters were supportive, but the ones that weren't penetrated deep into my soul. The few that couldn't hide their negativity left me feeling rejected. The feelings of rejection lingered, while supportive gestures only seemed to provide a temporary respite from my anxiety.

It had started to feel like I was on a roller coaster every time I went to Theta events. The highs could be so high—the friendships I had established with many of the Thetas in my pledge class kept me coming back. We had been through so much together in our first three years of college and were closer than any female friends I had ever had—by far. I was proud to be part of this close-knit family since I rushed my freshman year and felt a closeness to my sisters that I'd never felt before with any female friends.

But the lows could be so low—the rejection I felt from some Thetas, and my growing impatience and dissatisfaction with parties that revolved around frat guys left me feeling unsettled and conflicted. I could no longer feign interest in hooking up with guys. The pressure to wear pastels and feminine outfits wore me out, when I wanted to wear more boyish clothes. The conformity felt stifling. Avoidance and silence from many sisters made me feel rejected, or merely tolerated. It was a stark contrast with how I felt at GLBA: accepted, understood, seen, and celebrated for exactly who I really was. I saw my sorority differently than I had before. I often left events feeling emotionally exhausted and tonight was no different.

26

CLIT CLUB

June, Junior Year

I clenched the steering wheel of Valentina's old burgundy Oldsmobile. Cars honked at me and taxis swerved around me, cutting me off or passing me by. We were on a GLBA expedition to New York City for a Pride event over the summer.

Sitting in the passenger seat, Valentina said, "Try to turn left at the next street."

I said, "I can't even get out of this lane. Everyone is cutting me off. I've never seen this much traffic before. How did I end up being the one driving when we got into the city?"

Patches yelled from the backseat, "I can't wait to get out of this car! We've been in here for 16 hours!"

The narrow Manhattan streets were crammed with hordes of people during rush hour. A cyclist whizzed past me on the left. A warm wind of sour trash blew in through the windows. The dizzying array of lights and colors from street signs, shops, cars, and people made my eyes hurt. My hands were cramping up from holding the wheel so tight and my shoulders and neck burned from the tension.

I yelled, "These drivers are so rude!"

From the backseat, Barrett said, "You just need to be more aggressive."

After more than two hours navigating the city streets, we finally made it to our hotel in downtown Manhattan. The valet took Valentina's car to the garage. The sound of honks and yelling drivers still rang in my ears. Inside the hotel lobby, several small groups milled about. Some wore "freedom rings"—a necklace with six metal rings, one of each color of the rainbow—around their necks, or rainbow flag buttons on their backpacks.

Sideburns said, "I can't believe there are gay couples here holding hands in public!"

Barrett said, "I know! And there are gay people everywhere!" He pointed across the lobby. "Look at that hot guy over there with the blond hair."

Valentina leaned in, touching my arm, and whispered in my ear, "Barrett is so funny. He's always on the lookout for a hookup." Still holding on to my arm, she grinned.

Electricity shot through me as I remembered all the nights over the past couple of months when Valentina and I dirty danced together at Fallout. Valentina's curvy yet petite body moved in sync with mine, her arms wrapped around my waist as we gyrated to the pulsing music. I felt a little guilty enjoying it so much, but everybody else was grinding with each other so I tried not to think about it. I had seen a lot of Valentina last semester in GLBA, although nothing sexual had happened. Sarah was often busy and rarely went to GLBA or Fallout.

Toward the end of junior year, I had started to have doubts about my relationship with Sarah. We didn't see each other very often because she was so busy with swim team practice, her performance in the musical *Hair,* and her friends. Even though my schedule was packed too—with Theta, my part-time job conducting research with bipolar and schizophrenic subjects, and training as a peer counselor and rape hotline counselor—I always found myself wanting more from her.

We'd also had some conflict over sex. While I had orgasms almost every time, she only did sometimes. I often felt guilty and inadequate that I couldn't fully satisfy her. I knew she hadn't orgasmed with anyone before me, including her long-term boyfriend from high school, but it still created a dark cloud that I couldn't shake. And while I was excited to perform oral sex on her, she wasn't comfortable doing the same for me.

After a month apart from Sarah over the summer, thoughts of her had started to fade from my mind a little.

I entered our tiny hotel room with my friends from GLBA: Valentina, Barrett, Patches, and Sideburns. We were undeterred by the sole double bed and tossed our sleeping bags on the floor and began to squeeze into the tiny bathroom one at a time. It took a few hours before we were all showered and ready to go out.

Sarah's parents dropped her off while we were all getting ready. I hadn't seen her since school had ended and it seemed like an eternity. I expected to feel excited to see her, but instead I felt conflicted.

When we arrived at the Clit Club, a sign outside the door said CELEBRATE STONEWALL'S 25TH ANNIVERSARY AT THE CLIT CLUB! GIRL PARTY! Dozens of girls were in line outside the entrance: a girl with a nose ring, tattoos covering her arms, dark makeup, and punk clothes; butch women with black leather, black boots, and wallet chains; four beautiful femmes with long hair, lipstick, tight jeans, heels, and cleavage spilling out of tight tank tops; a pretty androgynous girl with short hair smoking a cigarette. I couldn't take my eyes off of them all. I had never seen so many lesbians before.

We walked into the dark, packed club filled with cigarette smoke and perfume. The walls, ceilings, and floor were all painted black. As we turned a corner, a huge dance floor opened up to us, hundreds of women collectively throbbing to the music, a handful of gay men dancing flamboyantly. Two hot women with long hair danced on the stage, one wrapped in an American flag and the other a rainbow flag, with nothing on under the flags. As they gyrated, moving the flags around, different parts of their smooth, toned skin were revealed.

The six of us swayed in the crowd. I could feel shoulders pressed against me. Black, white, Asian, Latina, femme, butch, punk, long hair, spiky short hair, piercings, boots, heels, lipstick, and breasts mesmerized me. Women sipped drinks and smoked cigarettes. Women made out, grinding with each other on the dance floor, radiating self-confidence.

Sarah bobbed to the music in baggy Gap jeans and a plain T-shirt. She wore no makeup and looked like an average Midwestern girl, in sharp contrast to the edgy, glamorous women we danced beside. Maybe it was our time apart or my growing exposure to other gay people, but I suddenly saw Sarah in a different light. The novelty of the burlesque dancers onstage and hordes of lesbians pulled my gaze away from Sarah.

I found myself not wanting to grind with Sarah with abandon like I pictured we would, now that we finally could. Finally, I was free to do so, and I felt inhibited—but now for a different reason. Guilt slapped me in the face as I felt drawn to the diversity of lesbians around me, to what I didn't know existed until that night. A sinking feeling crept over me as I started to notice feelings of attraction to others. We danced together, but I was distracted.

After about an hour Sarah leaned in and yelled, "I'm about ready to go. Are you?"

"Oh, I'm actually having a really good time and would love to stay. Are you sure?"

"Yeah. I'm just tired from the drive. And it's really loud."

The others stayed, but Sarah and I caught a cab back to the hotel room. I laid out two sleeping bags on the floor in the small space between the bed and the wall and we squished in together. We made out for a bit, but didn't do much beyond that. Sarah fell asleep while I lay staring at the ceiling, replaying scenes from the Clit Club. I thought about the burlesque dancers and the sexy women in tight tank tops and lipstick. The seemingly endless types of women made me feel a little less enthusiastic about Sarah. Guilt immediately punched me. At some point, the others came in drunk and passed out. I fell asleep shortly after.

The next morning, on June 26, 1994, we all walked to where the Pride parade started. The parade that year commemorated the 25th anniversary of the Stonewall riots in Manhattan, a series of spontaneous, violent demonstrations by members of the LGBT community against a police raid that took place in the early morning hours of June 28, 1969, at the Stonewall Inn in Greenwich Village— widely considered the most important event leading to the gay liberation movement and the modern fight for LGBT rights in the United States.

We were surrounded by tens of thousands of gay people wearing pink boas, rainbow-colored sequined hot pants, leather chaps, and drag queens in heavy makeup. People talked loudly, gesticulated wildly, and wore huge smiles. Women kissed other women. Guys had their hands in other guys' back pockets. Same-sex couples proudly strode arm in arm or hand in hand.

Protesters lined the streets holding signs that said GOD HATES FAGS, HOMOSEXUALITY IS A SIN, and GAYS ARE GOING TO HELL. As they yelled profanities at us, we quickened our steps to get past them.

Street vendors sold rainbow everything: T-shirts, bandannas, freedom rings, dog tags, hot pants, and baseball hats. Not one cloud crossed the sky that day. The sun warmed the city. Tens of thousands of gay people marched in the parade, holding a long rainbow flag over their heads. The flag stretched down the street as far as we could see, the brilliant sun reflecting against its colors. Hot guys and girls danced on floats in very little clothing. Festive party music pumped through the air. Women wore pasties on their nipples, or painted stars, or simply let their bare breasts move freely. One woman had painted a bikini onto her top and bottom with purple liquid latex. Guys revealed extremely muscled torsos.

I felt tears of joy welling up in my eyes as I took in the scene. I thought back to the year before, when sneaking into a musty basement on Friday nights to meet at most a dozen gay students was the highlight of my week. I had never imagined the ultimate celebration, color, pride, and diversity from the LGBTQ community that I now saw surrounding me.

I couldn't believe that just a year ago I had only met a handful of gay people, wasn't sure I was even bisexual, and had never even kissed a woman. I couldn't help but wonder how much sooner I would have come out and how much angst and drunken hookups with guys I could have avoided if I had known this type of community existed.

After the parade, we all walked to a big park for the concert and after party. Thousands lounged on the grass, holding drinks, snacking on hot dogs, and watching the bands onstage.

Sarah and I sat on the grass by ourselves. She wore shorts and a baggy T-shirt. I pulled at the grass beside me, tossing it aside. All day I had tried to avoid looking like we were together. I felt sick knowing I was pulling away. Now that I had seen what else was beyond the dozen gay people at Wash U, I suddenly wanted more than what Sarah and I had. I felt excited by the other possibilities and had to admit to myself that these feelings had been building since I had first become attracted to Valentina.

Sarah looked at me with concern and said, "I feel like you're not being as affectionate with me as you normally are."

I had tried to stuff my feelings since she arrived, but I felt conflicted and couldn't pretend any longer. We were out of earshot of my GLBA friends—the first time we'd been alone since the day she arrived. What I blurted out next was not planned.

"I'm just having a hard time with things. With us. It's hard with us not seeing each other over the summer. I know we already talked about not being exclusive, but maybe we should take a break from dating over the summer. Until we get back."

I looked up. She stared at me, but didn't say anything.

She cried. I cried too. After talking for a while, she decided to have her mom pick her up and take her home to Rochester. As I watched her walk away, I felt both deep sadness and a sense of relief. Guilt penetrated my soul. *Did I make a mistake?* A few tears rolled down my face. I wiped them away as I trudged back to my friends. I told them what happened and they hugged me. *What have I done?* I already missed her.

When it started to get dark, we walked back to our hotel, where we all freshened up. That night, we hit a gay bar called the Crow Bar. I needed many drinks after the conversation with Sarah. I felt awful, sick to my stomach from hurting her and overcome with a deep sadness. We drank and danced the night away.

On the drive back to St. Louis, Valentina's car broke down in a small town in Pennsylvania. She didn't have enough money to pay for the repairs, so Barrett offered his credit card. We stayed that night in a motel, with a couple 12-packs of beer and some rum and Coke.

After we settled into our motel for the night, Barrett yelled, "Let's play 'I Never'! One person starts and says something that they have never done. Like if I started, I could say, 'I never have had sex with a girl.' Then, anyone who has had sex with a girl has to drink, and tell their story if someone asks. Valentina, you start."

Valentina, shifting in her seat, said, "I've never kissed a guy." Barrett, Sideburns, and I drank.

Barrett then said, "I never had sex with someone on the roof of a frat house." I shot Barrett a dirty look and drank.

Patches said, "What? Story!"

I shrugged and said, "I was with Jake in the Hat and we were drunk after a party. For some reason we went up the ladder to the roof and had sex. Right in the middle of it the president of his fraternity came up the ladder and caught us! I have no idea why this guy was on the roof. I hardly cared because I was so wasted."

I looked at Barrett and said, "I've never had sex with two guys at the same time."

Barrett drank and shot me a big smile across the room.

Our game morphed into Truth or Dare, and I found myself hoping someone would dare Valentina to kiss me, or vice versa. No luck.

We made it home to St. Louis the next night. Valentina dropped me off at the apartment I was subletting over the summer, which felt very empty and cold now. Alone, I crawled into bed. I began to replay my conversation with Sarah in New York. Thinking about her crying made me start to cry. I thought about feeding her honeydew melon for the camera at the formal. I thought about our first kiss outside the laundry room of her dorm. I thought about our slow dance to "In Your Eyes." I thought about all the hours we'd spent talking on the phone and all the nights we'd spent having sex. I thought about the first time we said, "I love you." I thought about her smile and electrifying touch. I thought about how we navigated the coming out process together. I sobbed over the end of my most profound love, until I could barely catch my breath. When I stopped sobbing, I felt deeply exhausted. As I stared at the ceiling, I thought about my GLBA friends and felt a glimmer of hope for the future.

PART FOUR

SENIOR YEAR

27

NATIONAL COMING OUT DAY

September–October, Senior Year

For National Coming Out Day—October 11, a day to celebrate lesbian, gay, bisexual, and transgender people coming out—the GLBA leaders were hoping we could all wear T-shirts as a group. But at an early September meeting, most of us were uncomfortable with the idea.

The new GLBA president said, "I know it's uncomfortable, but this is to help others. There are tons of people on campus who are still in the closet. They need to see us being proud of who we are—and it's a chance for all of us to fully come out. If we do it together it'll be easier."

He paused, looking hopefully at the 14 fearful faces of people who hadn't volunteered yet. Alex wasn't at the meeting and neither was Sarah. Once Sarah came back to St. Louis for the start of school, we had many intense and tearful conversations, and off-again on-again time together. We were still together—not exclusively, though, and things felt different. I still loved Sarah, but continued to experience conflicted feelings of wanting to be close to her while also feeling occasional attractions to other women.

As the president scanned the room, I felt his gaze on me. I looked away. Visions of myself walking around campus with a NATIONAL COMING OUT DAY T-shirt on were like something out of a horror movie. I pictured myself walking alone across campus while people glared at me with anger, disgust, and confusion. From all directions, dozens of faces swarmed around me, closing in. I tried to get away, but couldn't escape. As people got closer, they laughed and pointed at me.

Then I heard, "Kristin, what about you?" His words catapulted me back into the room. The president looked expectantly at me. The group was silent. Curious eyes peered at me.

Disappointment in myself washed over me, for not having the courage to stand with the four others who were willing to wear the T-shirts. The thought of being openly out on campus made me feel sick, but the thought of not being brave enough to also sickened me.

It was the same sick feeling I'd felt when I struggled over dancing with Sarah: sick with fear about openly dancing with her, and sick with disappointment in myself for not being strong enough to stand up for who I was. Or when I struggled over adding Sarah's name to the list of guests, or when Sarah and I walked in to my formal together. Every time I came out to someone, I felt it too.

I was sick of feeling sick. Under the harsh fluorescent lighting, my hand suddenly shot up in the air and I said forcefully, "I'll do it."

Helen and Andy then reluctantly said they would wear a shirt as well. After more silence, it was clear nobody else would cave in. John, a GLBA leader, spoke up. "Okay, thanks guys. It looks like we've got seven people so far. I'll reach out to others in the group who weren't here today and to the leader of LBQ to see if they want to participate as well. I'll order extra T-shirts in case people change their minds."

"And while we're at it, please talk to anyone you think might be willing to appear in *Stud Life*." *Stud Life* was the Wash U student newspaper, published every week. "I'd like us to have a full-page spread listing people's names on campus who are gay or allies and willing to have their name in print—students, faculty, staff, and grad students. I'd also like to have people on campus write articles about their experiences coming out. Let me know if you're willing to do either, and spread the word!"

How is he going to convince people to put their name in print or write an article?

After the meeting, John walked over to me and asked if I would be willing to write an article. "I feel like you have such a unique story because you're in a sorority."

I stood in silence for a moment, unable to move or speak. "Um, no, I don't think so. I don't really know how to write. I'm sorry—I really wish I could help, but I just don't think so."

"I understand. If you change your mind, let me know."

The tapping of students' keystrokes filled the computer lab on campus. Each table held a desktop PC, monitor, and keyboard. At 11 p.m., a couple dozen students still sat, working away.

I typed a few sentences, then retyped them, multiple times, veering from sadness to elation as I reflected on my coming-out journey over the past couple years. I struggled with the right words as I vividly imagined people reading and reacting to them.

Stuck, I sat back in my chair and stuffed my hands in the pockets of my green Wash U sweatshirt. I stared at the screen. The words got blurrier the longer I looked at them. After a few moments, more words came to me. I typed, deleted, then typed and deleted again.

I thought to myself, *Why did I let John convince me to write an article?* Even though I was terrified of coming out so publicly, after first saying no I had felt something push me forward. I felt powerful and courageous writing the story. It felt like the right thing to do—to stand up for who I was and to help others on campus who struggled with their sexual orientation just like I did. I felt a sense of release putting my experiences in writing.

I had already spent a few weeks trying to craft it and it was due the next morning, so tonight was my last push.

Feeling stuck again, I walked out of the computer lab and down a long hall. When I arrived at the vending machines, I put two quarters in and pressed the big red button for Coke. I reached in for the cold can, then turned to the food vending machine. I looked at the rows of Doritos, Cheetos, Snickers, Kit Kats, and cookies. *Should I get animal crackers or M&Ms?* I took another two quarters out of my pocket and fed them in, then grabbed my plain M&Ms and walked back to the computer lab.

I sat back down at my PC, pulled open the bag of M&Ms, and took one out. I popped it in my mouth and slowly munched on it, then took a sip of the sweet, fizzy Coke.

Staring at the screen, I thought, *I know some Thetas don't want people to know there is a lesbian in their sorority. How are my sisters going to react to me talking about coming out within Theta? Can I really do this?*

The only thing I'd ever had published was a poem in my high school literary publication. Sure, I took one class in fiction writing in college and I was always an avid journal writer, but this was different. I knew my subject matter would be shocking to most people.

At 1 a.m. I felt finished—enough. I pulled a large black plastic floppy disk out of my blue Jansport backpack and fed it into the drive, saving it. When the red light on the disk drive turned from red to green, I ejected my disk and carefully placed it in its protective sleeve.

I sat for a few minutes staring at it. That disk held my ultimate coming out. I felt hopeful that I could finally shake the sick feeling, but at the same time I was terrified.

• • •

On the morning of October 11, 1994 I woke up early, even without an alarm. I had tossed and turned most of the night, plagued by worries about people's reaction to my article.

I rolled off my futon mattress, grabbed an Eddie Bauer plaid flannel shirt, and buttoned it up.

Once I got to campus, I immediately walked to the Student Union. I grabbed a plain bagel and orange juice, then looked to where I knew a basket of *Stud Life* newspapers was located—about 50 feet away. I stared as student after student stooped down, grabbed a paper, reading it as they walked away.

Someone said, "Excuse me" and I turned around. I was standing in the way of the food line.

I headed for the newspapers, laser-focused on them. When I got there, I quickly grabbed a paper from the basket. Then I found the first empty bench in the Student Union and sat down to read it.

The black-and-white newspaper shook in my hands. I knew that almost everyone read it cover to cover. Realistically, I could expect that most of my fellow students would read my article.

I unfolded it and quickly scanned the front page. No mention of National Coming Out Day, any gay-related topics, or my article. I opened the paper to pages 2–3. Hands shaking, I scanned these pages as well. Again, no mention of anything gay.

Then I opened the paper to pages 4–5.

In huge bold letters on page 4: SORORITY GROWS TO ACCEPT LESBIAN SISTER. Underneath the title in large letters was KRISTIN GRIFFITH, and below that, STUDENT PERSPEC-TIVE. Underneath that a pull-quote: "Don't even dare think your sorority or fraternity has no lesbians, bisexuals, or gays, because it does. Think about it the next time you call your brother a faggot. What if he is?"

Upon seeing my article spanning pages 4–5 and continuing on to page 7, my bagel threatened to come up. I took some deep breaths to calm the nausea. I looked around at all the students walking around carrying newspapers.

After a few more deep breaths, I dove back into my article. Although I had read it many times when editing it, I needed to read it again.

Some of the phrases I wrote now jumped out at me. The article started with "What's it like being an out lesbian in a sorority?" It ended with, "Think about what you say, because chances are that you may be hurting some of your sorority sisters and fraternity brothers when you make homophobic comments or aren't willing to be accepting of a homosexual brother or sister. Think about it— because believe me, it hurts to hear homophobic comments from your friends, your sorority sisters, and your fraternity brothers. For many, the sorority or fraternity may provide a sort of family for members, and who wants to be made to feel like dirt by your own family?" Seeing my words in print brought back all the times I'd heard a frat guy call one of his brothers a "fagatron" or "fairy" or a sorority girl call someone a "lesbo" or "dyke."

I wrote about the stress of attending date functions as a gay woman. "Something that made me anxious about taking my girlfriend was an experience a lesbian here at WU had told me about. She had been invited to a date function at a sorority by one of her friends who happened to be heterosexual. She described how her friend's sorority sisters didn't talk to her while she was there, making her and her friend feel very unwelcome and uncomfortable. And they weren't even a couple."

Reading this made me remember that I had legitimate reasons for concern around coming out to my sorority. I often berated myself for not being courageous enough, for being scared just to be myself—but being out so publicly brought home that it wasn't all in my head.

After reading my article, I flipped through the rest of the newspaper, looking for other articles related to National Coming Out Day. The only other thing I saw was a half-page ad listing the names of a few dozen people who were gay or allies. We couldn't even get enough names to fill an entire page.

I closed the newspaper and put it in my backpack. I tentatively got up, my senses on high alert. I felt like I was lost alone in the jungle at night, my ears perked up for the sound of leaves crunching underneath the feet of a wolf, or the heavy breath of a tiger. I strained my eyes for any sign of dangerous movement. Every sound was a predator ready to pounce, every movement a deadly snake or scorpion.

I walked out into the brisk air and brilliant sunshine, and headed for my first class. I saw someone I knew from my sorority coming straight toward me on the path, and wondered if she'd read the article. It was only 10 a.m.; maybe she hadn't yet.

As she approached, I avoided eye contact and hoped she wouldn't notice me. No such luck.

"Hey, Kristin!"

"Hey," I said timidly.

She stopped and said, "I read your article."

I froze. Was this a snake about to dig its fangs into my leg?

The girl said, "It was great. I really enjoyed it."

I stood in stunned silence. Unable to move, I just looked at her. I managed to open my mouth. "Oh, thank you." As she walked off, I just stood there staring.

Walking around campus throughout the day, a handful of other people from my sorority, some of whom I had never had a substantive conversation with before, had similar comments. "That must have taken a lot of courage to write." "I'm glad you wrote it."

With each positive comment, my fears and insecurities lessened. My fight or flight response began to be overtaken by more positive feelings. I started to notice the beautiful sunshine, the cottony clouds, and birds flying between trees filled with crimson leaves. I felt a little pep in my step as I walked between classes. I felt a little taller, more hopeful, less alone.

About a week after National Coming Out Day, Nikki, the president of my sorority, came up to me after our weekly sorority chapter meeting. "Hey, do you have a minute to talk?"

"Um, sure."

"Let's go over there, where we can have some privacy." She motioned to a far corner where nobody was sitting.

Nikki and I had taken many women's studies classes together, and once she had confided in me that she thought she might be bisexual. She said nobody else knew. She had a thick Southern accent and oozed charm.

We sat, and her face showed concern. She leaned in and said quietly, "So, I wanted to let you know about something that happened last week during the weekly sorority president's meeting. A few of the chapter presidents brought up your article. They asked the group if anyone knew what sorority you were in, since you didn't say in the article."

I had decided not to disclose which sorority I was in, for fear of angering my sisters. I knew some would feel ashamed to have a lesbian in their sorority and wouldn't want others to know.

She paused. I listened and waited for her to continue.

"I knew, of course, but wasn't sure whether to say anything. Anyway, I decided to tell them you were in Theta."

"Oh, what did they say?"

"Well, there was a discussion about the image of sororities on campus. I just want you to know that I'm really proud of you. Yeah, not everyone is happy about it, but I do support you. I'm going to post the article in the sorority suite, in case anyone missed it."

I avoided going to the suite while it was posted. While a few of my sisters had shared positive feedback, the silence from more than 75 other sisters made me feel on edge. Though I had truly felt like I belonged before I figured out I was gay, once I didn't fit the straight, feminine mold I never really felt like I fully belonged again. The silences, the lack of interest or excitement about my crushes or relationships with women, the continued assumption that everyone wanted to bring a male date to every function left little space for me. The subtle messages that being straight and feminine was the ideal were woven throughout the fabric of the sorority-fraternity mixers, and the culture. The newfound strength I felt from expressing myself more fully was clouded by a deep sadness at the loss of belonging in Theta.

28

HOT FOR TEACHER

November, Senior Year

"All behavior is really just a complex series of conditioned responses to stimuli. All behavior, even human behavior, can be explained by the principles of pleasure and pain. Organisms seek pleasure and avoid pain."

I sat in my Psychology of Learning class, mesmerized as Professor Schwartz spoke. At the front of the small class of about 30 students, I scribbled copious notes and absorbed her every word. Professor Schwartz had close-cropped dark brown hair and wore a maroon long-sleeve shirt with three buttons undone at the top, and tight jeans.

"Rats can be trained to do just about anything if the right rewards and punishments are applied. The real dilemma comes when they cannot predict whether they will receive a reward or a punishment after a particular behavior."

She strode confidently across the front of the classroom, making eye contact with everyone individually as she spoke with assurance

and animation. Her green eyes pulled me in. She gestured passionately, turning rat experiments into fascinating stories, capturing my
attention.

My pen moved quickly over my blue college-ruled notebook,
my writing almost illegible as I stared at her. She spoke quickly
and enthusiastically, looking directly at us.

"There is a famous psychology experiment about learned helplessness that holds some important lessons about animal and human
behavior. Three groups of dogs were placed in harnesses. Group
one dogs were simply placed in harnesses and later released. This
was the control group. Group two dogs were placed in harnesses
and given electrical shocks to cause pain. However, when group
two dogs pressed a lever, they could stop the electrical shocks.
These dogs learned to press the lever to escape the painful shocks.
Group three dogs were placed in harnesses and wired in parallel
with group two dogs. They experienced shocks of the same intensity
and duration of the group two dogs. However, group three dogs had
no control over the shocks. Their levers had no effect."

She stopped. "What do you think happened to the dogs after the
experiment?"

Silence filled the classroom. Her long eyelashes framed her luminescent eyes.

"Nobody has a guess?"

A girl behind me raised her hand.

"Yes, Heather."

"The group one dogs were fine, while the group two and three
dogs were injured and stressed because they got shocked?"

"Good guess. You are partially correct. Group one dogs were
fine, just as you said. Group two dogs quickly recovered after the

experiment as well. However, the dogs from group three exhibited symptoms similar to clinical depression in humans after the experiments."

Professor Schwartz paused. I heard the scratching of pencils and pens on paper. "Can anyone guess why?"

Silence again.

"The reason group three dogs were so negatively affected was because of the combination of the unpredictability of the shocks AND the fact that they had no control over them. The dogs couldn't stop the shocks. Nothing they did had any effect."

She then continued with, "Does anyone know how this might apply to humans? Can you think of an example?"

Her question made me think of my whole coming out experience. Though I wasn't depressed, I certainly felt stressed a lot, on edge, vulnerable. I never knew how someone might react and I felt like I had no control over it. Some people were supportive. Some people became distant. Some people couldn't hide their look of disgust or fear or awkwardness. I always felt apprehensive, not knowing what someone's reaction would be and knowing I had no control over it. On top of that, coming out was something I had to do continually. It wasn't once and done.

I remained silent, but someone eventually spoke up.

I hung on Professor Schwartz's every word. I had heard that she'd won an award for best teacher of the year. There are hundreds of teachers at Wash U and she was by far the best I had ever had.

With only a few minutes left in our class, Professor Schwartz said, "Our next class will be optional. Instead of our regular class, let's meet in the Pub and I'll buy everyone a beer. It will be an informal class, more discussion than anything. I hope to see you there."

• • •

As I neared the Rat that Friday afternoon, I hesitated, feeling a tingling in my toes, and slowly opened the heavy wood door. The smell of stale beer wafted into my nostrils and I stepped into the dark amber glow.

The small bar opened up into a seating area with tables scattered about, the low ceilings giving the bar a cozy feeling. Sunlight from a few small windows saturated the wood tables and cast long shadows throughout the bar. The bar was almost empty, except for a group of about seven students sitting in a circle, facing Professor Schwartz. Pint glasses of foamy beer were scattered across the table. Professor Schwartz moved her hands quickly as she explained something, smiling broadly as she spoke.

I stood there for a moment, took a deep breath, then timidly walked toward the group. There was an empty seat next to the professor. People were probably scared to sit next to her. I was too.

As she continued to speak, I slowly slid into the seat next to her. She stopped momentarily, smiled at me, and said "Hi, Kristin."

"Hey." I wondered if she could hear the shakiness in my voice.

She continued explaining something to another student, laughing a few times. I couldn't seem to pay attention to what she was saying.

The tall bartender came over to the table and said, "Anyone want anything?"

The professor asked, "Kristin, can I get you a beer? Anyone ready for another?"

"Sure, I'll take one," I said.

A couple of the other students asked for another.

Professor Schwartz said, "Okay, four beers."

When it arrived, I took a sip of my cold beer, which tasted delicious. Professor Schwartz sipped hers too as students continued to ask her questions. She seemed to have an answer for everything. She oozed confidence, commanding everyone's attention.

She wore tight jeans, like she always did, with a hunter-green shirt. *Could she be gay? She looks like she could be. She has never mentioned a husband or kids like many professors do.*

I could feel the energy of her body next to mine. I couldn't contain the attraction I felt to her. A thrilling sensation coursed through me, making my fingers tingle. Too tongue-tied to say anything, I just listened, continued to sip my beer, and gazed at her. *I hope she can't tell how un-self-confident I am right now.*

At 4 p.m., students started to leave. I asked her a question about one of the readings right as the last two people were leaving. She turned to face me, smiled, and started to describe the results of a rat experiment that highlighted the concept I had asked about. I already knew the experiment and understood the concept. I just wanted to keep her there.

I didn't hear any of her answer. Her intensity mesmerized me. After she finished her explanation, she stopped, then took a sip of her beer. "Do you have any other questions? Otherwise class is over and you're free to go."

Think fast, think fast. My pint glass was about a third full and hers was almost empty. I suddenly realized we were the only two people left in the bar, other than the bartender. My heart beat faster as a moment of silence passed between us.

She turned her chair slightly to face me. "So, what do you think of the class?"

Mid-sip, I awkwardly swallowed my beer. "This is my favorite class. You make it really interesting. I mean, I didn't think rat experiments could be so cool." *Did that sound stupid? I can't believe I said rat experiments were cool!*

"I'm so glad. I love teaching this class." She beamed.

I could see she had just finished the last of her beer. Only a little foam remained on the bottom of her glass. My hand shook as I downed the last of mine. *Can she see my hand shaking?*

We got up and I followed her out. She opened the door and sunlight streamed in; she stepped outside and I followed her. Outside, she turned to face me. We both squinted in the bright afternoon light. The trees had started to turn and crimson leaves lay scattered all over the stone pathway. A light breeze rustled through the trees and bushes.

"Thanks for coming today. I was glad people showed up even though class was optional."

"Um, yeah, thanks. It was really fun." I paused, searching for words to prolong our conversation. "Yeah, and thanks for the beer."

"Absolutely! Have a great weekend and I'll see you in class next week."

"Um, yeah, you too." As I turned to walk away, my legs felt like Jell-O, weak and wobbly.

Nervous energy coursed through my veins as I walked toward the psychology building. A few puffy white clouds floated in the blue sky. The trees had lost all their leaves now. It was two weeks before finals.

I arrived at the tall gothic style brick building and hesitated at the grand front door.

Over the past few days, I'd racked my brain to find an excuse to go to Professor Schwartz's office hours—I'd never been to office hours for her class or any other. After a lot of thought, I'd come up with a few questions, but as I stood outside the building, I couldn't remember them. After a few moments, I managed to remember one. A frigid breeze whipped through my hair, seeping into the top of my coat.

I hesitated, then quickly pulled open the heavy wood door, and stepped in. The warmth hit me as the door closed behind me with a *whoosh.*

As I turned right, blocking my way to Professor Schwartz's office stood white double doors—and they were locked. There was a keypad on the wall, but she hadn't said anything about needing a code.

As I stood there, I felt like I was stepping off a ledge into the unknown. I stared at the door, waited, then finally gently knocked on the door. I fidgeted, pulling my hands in and out of my jeans' pockets. I waited a few more moments.

I knocked again, this time harder. Suddenly, I heard a *click* and the door opened.

Professor Schwartz stood only inches from me. Fire filled my body.

"Hey! Come on in. Are you here for office hours?"

"Yeah, I am."

I followed her as she turned right into an open door. As I stepped inside, she sat down at a desk cluttered with papers, books, and piles of files. Shelves lined every wall of the large office space, psychology books spilling out. The whole impression was of an intelligent mess.

We were alone. I stood just inside the door. She sat facing me, looking at me expectantly. "So, how are you? How can I help you?"

She smiled and leaned back in her chair, looking relaxed. She wore her usual tight jeans and a form-fitting, long-sleeve button-down.

"Good. I just had a question about something for our final." *Can she hear the nervousness in my voice?*

"Sure, what can I help you with?" She leaned forward. "You can sit down if you like." She pointed to the chair just a few inches from hers.

I slowly moved toward her and sat down. We faced each other, our knees almost touching.

What was my question? I'd spent so much energy trying to come up with intelligent-sounding questions, so she'd be impressed. "Um, can you go over the experiment you went over in the last class again?"

"Oh, yes." She enthusiastically spoke for a few minutes. I watched her lips and the variety of expressions that crossed her face. She stopped and said, "Does that make sense?"

"Yeah, thanks." I paused briefly, then blurted out, "I also really wanted to thank you for the beer the other day. Um, so, do you usually go out for beers at the Pub?"

"Occasionally. What about you?"

"Yeah. I usually go most Thursday nights." *I wonder if I can figure out if she's gay.* I quickly asked, "Do you go out for drinks at other places?"

"Sometimes, but not that often. I'm working on finishing my dissertation, so I spend most of my free time on that. You?"

"Um, sometimes I go off campus, to places like Fallout and Probe." I dropped the names of gay bars to see her reaction.

"I've been to Probe a few times with some of my friends."

She could be gay, or she could just be a fag hag. Sitting so close to her, I could feel the energy radiating off her body. Her intense eye contact drilled straight into my core.

I anxiously glanced at my watch. "Oh, sorry. I just noticed office hours are over. I'm so sorry to keep you! Um, well, thanks for explaining. I really appreciate it."

"Oh, no problem at all. Happy to help. Good luck in your studying. I expect you'll do great. You're doing very well in the class so far."

She knows how I'm doing? Does she know how everyone is doing?

I studied so hard for that final. I took notes on everything in the book, summarized all the main points from my class notes, and reread everything. *I'm going to get an A on this final.* I spent hours and hours in the library.

Two weeks later, I walked into the classroom feeling ready. After two and a half hours of an all-essay final, I was happy with it and turned my blue book into the proctor at the front of the classroom, the first person to finish.

As I walked out of the room, Professor Schwartz happened to be in the hall. She said, "Hi, Kristin." My heart stopped.

"Hi."

"Done already? How do you think you did?"

Her exams were known to be very difficult and they were always all-essay. There were no multiple-choice questions to make it easier.

"I think I did well. Well, I hope I did." I smiled shyly.

"Okay, good. Enjoy your break. Are you going anywhere?"

"I'm going to Jackson Hole, Wyoming, to spend Christmas with my family. What are you doing?"

"I'll actually be staying here for a while to work on my dissertation. Then I'll go back to New Jersey and visit my family for a bit." She paused, then said, "Well, have fun over break!"

"Yeah, you too!"

I almost tripped as I turned around. Then I walked out of the psychology building, smiling to myself. The gorgeous sun warmed my face and I heard birds chirping as they flew by.

I suddenly imagined kissing her in her office. *What makes you think that could really happen? You don't even know if she's gay. And why would she go out with a student?*

29

"A" IS FOR ATTRACTION

January, Senior Year

I stood in front of the psychology building on the first day of classes, picturing Professor Schwartz reading photocopied articles at her cluttered desk, underlining important phrases with a yellow highlighter. I replayed sitting next to her at the Pub drinking a beer, her passionate words in class, our conversation during office hours.

A couple of loud students passed beside me, pulling me out of my fantasy world. I walked away from the building, then stopped and turned around. I looked at the grand facade. My heart sped up.

Can I do this? What if I make a fool of myself? Is this a bad idea?

I had spent the three weeks over break planning exactly what I was going to say. This time I wasn't going to forget. I couldn't get her out of my head.

I felt like I might throw up. But I had to know. I wouldn't be able to stop thinking about her if I didn't know one way or the other.

Students passed by me in heavy down coats, hats with pom poms on top, and mittens. The stone pathways bustled with students walking to class, chatting with friends. A dusting of white snow covered the dead grass and I could see the fog of my breath in front of me as I exhaled.

Okay, it's time.

I walked to the door of the psych building. As the door opened it creaked ever so slightly. I entered and paused at the stairwell. The keypad to which I did not know the code stared at me. I took off my right mitten and gingerly knocked on the door, and waited for what seemed like eternity. Then, I waited some more. I knocked again, this time a little louder. I waited, staring at the door, uncertainty pumping harder through my body with every passing moment.

A male voice from behind me said, "Can I help you?"

I jumped and quickly spun around. Dr. Eisenberg, a tenured professor of the psychology of learning, stood with a perplexed look on his face. He wasn't much taller than me. "Oh, yes. I'm looking for Professor Schwartz. Is she around?"

He said, "She's out of the office until next week. Is there something I can help you with?"

"Oh, okay. Thanks. I can just come back later. Do you know what day she's coming back?"

"I believe on Monday."

"Okay, thanks."

I quickly walked past him, up the stairs, and out of the building. Shoulders slumped and head hanging low, I plodded across campus in the direction of my next class. *I have to endure another week of this torture?*

That same week, an envelope arrived in the mail from Wash U, at my three-bedroom off-campus apartment that I shared with Jake in the Hat and Jake's fraternity brother. I was 95 percent sure I knew what it was. It sat on top of our coffee table, littered with an ashtray and cigarette butts, the smell of stale smoke lingering in the air. A pizza box sat on the carpet next to the table, a bong lying on its side next to it. My roommates were such slobs.

I tore open the envelope, quickly scanning to find out what grade I had gotten in the Psychology of Learning. I got an A! Professor Schwartz had told our class that although not technically graded on a curve, most people would get a B or below, with only a few people in the A range. I did a quick hand pump in the air. Luckily, my roommates weren't around to see it.

It was now Monday morning, the day Professor Schwartz was supposed to be back. Revved up, I bounced off my futon.

Near the beginning of senior year, I had decided to cut off my long hair. I hadn't worn my hair short since about third grade, so cutting it was a big deal; I kept it long so I wouldn't stick out and make my lack of femininity even more obvious than it already was. I hesitated for months, but finally went to a salon where the hairdresser kept asking me if I was sure. Although scared to be the only woman in my sorority with hair as short as a guy's, I took the plunge. Right away, I immediately felt more "me" than I ever had with long hair. I was also hoping this would give me better luck with women, because maybe they would actually be able to tell I was gay! The first day I walked on campus with short hair, people I had been friends with since freshman year walked right past me—they didn't recognize me at all!

I quickly took a shower, brushed my teeth, and added some gel to my newly short, boyish hair. As I moved every hair where I wanted it, I smiled at myself in the mirror. I felt a new sense of confidence seeing a more androgynous, less feminine image of myself. I felt like my true self was finally reflected back at me.

I pulled on a pair of jeans, brown leather hiking/snow boots, and a sporty-looking striped crew-neck sweater that I had just gotten from my parents for Christmas.

Outside the front door, searing cold greeted me. I walked down the stairwell to my white Volkswagen Fox. Ice covered the windshield. I turned on the car and heater, then grabbed my ice scraper from the floor of the back seat. The scratching sound filled the air as I tried to slowly chip away at the ice. My ears stung from the cold. I wasn't wearing a hat, because I didn't want to mess up my hair that I had gotten just right. I never worried about this when I had long hair.

Eventually, I managed to get enough of the ice off to see through the front and back windows. I drove the ten minutes to campus, parked, and walked straight to the Student Union.

I got a coffee and a bear claw. The coffee cup warmed my fingers as I walked to a table and sat down. Only a few other students lingered in the café. Early morning light glittered off the trees through the large windows. I took a bite of the flaky bear claw and washed it down with a sip of coffee. Would Professor Schwartz be there today after I finished my first class? After eating about half of my bear claw, I began to feel nauseous from nerves and threw away the rest.

I sipped the rest of my coffee in my anthropology class, thoughts of Professor Schwartz racing through my mind. When class ended, I quickly packed up my stuff and walked to the psych building. I could feel the bear claw in my throat and felt like retching.

The doors to the offices were open. *I bet this means she's here.* Her door was just a few steps away, and it was open. I'd been imagining this moment for a month. *Okay, here goes.*

I slowly crept toward her door and peered around the corner. She sat at her desk, which was piled high with books and stapled articles, looking to be in deep concentration, like she was reading something.

I said "Hi."

She looked up and a stunned look swept across her face. She then smiled a wide smile. "Hey! How are you? I wasn't expecting to see you."

I smiled back. "Yeah, well, I was in the building and I thought I'd stop by and see if you were around." I wondered if she would believe this. I paused. My heart raced. *She can't hear it, right?*

"Well, it's good to see you. Come on in! How was your break?"

I walked in until I stood about five feet away from her. "Um, it was great. I met my family in Jackson Hole and did a lot of skiing." My sister had now been sober for a few years and was a sophomore at the University of Denver. After the initial shock sophomore year, it hadn't taken long for my sister and parents to accept that I was gay. I was lucky.

"That sounds fun."

I quickly blurted out, "So, I actually stopped by because I thought maybe I could buy you a beer sometime, to repay you." *Pound. Pound. Pound.* I could feel my heart reverberating through my whole body now.

A look of surprise appeared on her face. I clenched my fists tightly in the pockets of my jacket as I waited for her response.

She said, "Well, you definitely don't owe me a beer. It was really my pleasure. But, I would love to. I'll take you up on that."

I can't believe it! She just said yes!

Continuing, she said, "Here, I'll give you my home phone number in case you can't reach me here. Give me a call and we can grab a beer sometime."

She tore a corner off an article she was reading, scribbled something on it, and handed it to me. In messy handwriting it said "Erika" with two phone numbers listed. One said "office" and one said "home." I felt lightheaded.

In an upbeat voice, she said, "I've got to go to the lab and check on the rats. Come with me?"

"Sure."

I followed her down the long white hallway. Her hair, even shorter than mine, looked freshly cut. She stopped and pressed a few buttons on a keypad, and the door opened. As I followed her in, I immediately smelled rat feces. Metal cages packed the small room and lined the walls on all four sides. Rats filled the cages, stacked three or four high all around.

"Congratulations on getting an A in my class. You must've studied hard."

"I did." I felt myself blushing as she looked at me. I hoped it wasn't obvious.

She began checking dials on the rat cages and writing down what looked like numbers on a pad of paper. "So, do you think you might be interested in the psychology of learning for grad school?"

"I'm not sure. I was planning to apply to clinical psychology Ph.D. programs, but I ended up deciding not to. It just didn't feel quite right. I'll be looking for a job after graduation, and then will figure out what's next."

She weighed another rat on the scale and scribbled something in a notebook. Then she looked up and said, "It's probably good you went with your gut feeling."

We stood motionless, looking at each other.

She then said, "So, tell me, have you been to Probe or Fallout lately?"

"Um, no, but I was at Attitudes last weekend." This was the main lesbian dance club in St. Louis. *Now she for sure knows I'm gay.* I hoped dropping this clue might help me figure out if she was gay too.

"I haven't been there, but I've heard of it."

We walked out of the rat room and into the hallway. She turned to me and said, "I'm so glad you stopped by. And I really would love to grab a beer with you."

"Yeah, me too. Um, I'll talk to you soon then?"

"Sounds great."

I bounded up the stairs. My jittery hands shook inside my jacket pockets as I walked outside. *I can't believe my hot teacher actually wants to get a beer with me! How long should I wait before calling her? Should I play it cool and wait a few days, so I don't seem too eager?*

I managed to wait exactly one day. The next morning, I dialed her home phone. *Ring. Ring. Ring. Ring.* On the fourth ring her answering machine picked up.

"Hi, this is Erika. I'm not here now, so please leave a message."

I said, "Hi, um, this is Kristin. I was just calling to see when I could, um, buy you that beer I owe you. I'm actually going to be tied up at my sorority suite for rush pretty much all week and weekend, so here's that number too."

Click. I hung up and immediately started waiting for her to call back.

30

CALL ME

January, Senior Year

All 80 Thetas crammed into our sorority suite, squished on the couches, the long bench covered in a pastel floral print, the piano bench, on top of the coffee table, on chairs, and strewn about the floor. A sea of cable-knit sweaters, Theta sweatshirts, and ponytails packed the room. Shoulder-to-shoulder in the cozy space, we listened intently to Becky, our rush chair.

"We've just received the list of rushees that will be going through rush starting later this week. The first thing I will need all of you to do is look at the list. If you know any of the girls, whether from your hometown city or from the dorms or classes, then you will need to rate the girl on a scale of 1 to 10. If you feel she would make a great addition, give her a 10. If she would not fit in, give her a 1."

"If there are any special situations with any of the rushees, our two advisers from the national offices are here to help. If you know of a reason that any of these girls should not be admitted, like illegal drug use or anything else, please speak to one of our advisers.

They will keep the specific information you tell them completely confidential."

Becky handed out the list: rows of girls' names from the top to bottom and on the back. I started reading through the 350 names. I recognized only three other names on the list and gave them a 9, a 7, and a 6. Then I turned in my ballot.

Scratch, scratch, scratch went pens against paper. Fluorescent pinks, oranges, and yellows shone through the windows as sunset approached. One by one, girls shuffled across the room, carefully placing their folded votes in the ballot box on the coffee table. This was the first step in getting the best class of pledges.

I got up and walked to the kitchen area. I filled a small plastic cup with ice, poured myself a Coke, and grabbed two chocolate chip cookies. As I took a bite, I wondered about Professor Schwartz. I had left her a message that morning. *I wonder if she'll try calling me here.*

After another 30 minutes, everyone had finished voting. Becky spoke again. "So, now I'm going to explain exactly how the rush process works and then we're going to practice. Juniors and seniors are familiar with this, but for sophomores this will be new."

"For every party we will receive a list of names and the order in which they will enter the suite. We will all be lined up inside the suite waiting for the girls to enter. Most of you will be assigned one girl to intercept as she arrives; the rest of you not assigned to girls will be floaters. You are to join rushees, but never more than three of us to each one of them at a time. We want them to feel welcomed, but not overwhelmed."

"If you are assigned a rushee, you cannot leave that rushee until a floater has joined you. Only leave them at an appropriate time in the conversation. When you leave, the floater will stay with them until another floater joins her. A rushee should never ever be left alone. The goal is to have at least three of us meet each rushee. When you leave a rushee, go to the next girl on the list. Everyone will have name tags. Any questions?"

Someone asked, "How long should you stay with each girl?"

"About 15 to 20 minutes. There will be clocks on the walls. Don't look at your watch—we don't want the rushee to feel you're not interested. Make sure to ask them many questions and really try to learn something about them. And smile. Don't forget to smile. Any other questions?" Becky looked around the room and waited for other questions. "Okay, now we're going to practice!"

Groans spread throughout the room.

Some of us pretended to be rushees and we started to run through the flow, to make sure everyone knew where to go. We heard a loud knock on the sorority suite door. The girl closest to the door opened it. It was a pizza delivery. We all stopped what we were doing and started grabbing plates and napkins, then slices.

Once most people had finished eating, practice started again. Becky pulled me aside and said, "You don't need to practice since you're Computer Chair. Do you want to find Tina and start working on the votes?"

"Yes, great." I was excited when elected as Computer Chair and looked forward to avoiding small talk during the rush parties. My primary role was to manage the data behind the rigorous sorority recruitment process. I was getting a chance to see, behind the scenes, how girls got selected to join our sorority.

I grabbed the ballot box, then found Tina. She was wearing her baby blue KAΘ sweatshirt. I told her, "It's time for us to start working on the votes."

She followed me into the office, and I closed the door. I sat in the chair in front of the desk and she pulled up a chair next to the desk, facing me.

"So, let's enter the hometown votes first. Then we should at least start on all the other information on the girls. We've got to get all of that entered and get the initial rankings of everyone by Thursday." I took the top off the ballot box and set it next to Tina. "Do you want to read these to me, while I enter them in?"

"Sure."

I turned on the huge desktop Gateway PC and the screen flickered on. I clicked on an icon and opened the primitive database software, specifically designed for use by sororities. The Internet and email hadn't taken off yet.

When I was in elementary school, I liked to write simple computer programs in BASIC on my IBM PC Junior, displaying simple color pictures on the screen, like robots or houses. I spent hours writing code defining the location and color of every single pixel on the screen. After mastering that, I wrote simple programs that asked the user questions. Depending on the user's response, the computer would respond in ways that I defined. I had also taken one semester of computer programming in college. My experience with computers made me way overqualified for the position of Computer Chair.

Tina took the first ballot out of the box.

She scanned the first page, then said "Roxanne Clark. Eight. In the notes section it says 'We both live in the same dorm and are on the same intramural soccer team. She is sweet, good at soccer, and seems popular with the other girls.'"

I searched for Roxanne's name and typed the information in the appropriate boxes on the screen. I said, "Okay, done."

Tina looked back at her list and said, "Heather Young. Three. She wrote, 'She lives on my floor and keeps to herself a lot. She seems a little awkward and shy. Plus, she seems kind of uptight. I don't think she would fit in."

After about an hour, we switched. I read and Tina typed. Finally, we finished, and took a break.

I looked at my watch. Almost 8 p.m. and Professor Schwartz still hadn't called. *Maybe she called my home phone instead.* I could call my apartment and see if someone was home to check our answering machine. *What if she doesn't call? What if she doesn't really want to get a beer with me and was just being nice? I mean, why would a professor want to hang out with a college senior?*

I drained my Coke. Tina said, "Do you want to start on the background info?"

In the office sat a huge pile of 350 forms completed by the rushees. Another smaller pile contained the GPA, classes taken, and classes currently enrolled in, of all rushees from the registrar's office.

Tina picked up the first form, read the rushee name, then continued with information on hometown, college major, sports played, hobbies, clubs, high school GPA, SAT scores, leadership experience, and job experience. I typed all the information in, and we moved on to the next name. All of this data fed into the final score that each rushee received, which determined whether she would be invited back to parties and ultimately receive a bid to join.

After about 15 minutes in the cramped office, a loud ringing from the beige rotary phone startled us. My heart jumped. *What if it's Professor Schwartz?*

The phone rang again. I grabbed the plastic receiver out of the cradle. "Kappa Alpha Theta."

"Is Kristin there? Kristin Griffith?" said a woman's voice.

"Yes, this is Kristin."

"Hi, it's Erika."

I almost dropped the phone. "Oh, hi!" Tina gave me a quizzical look. "Um, can you hold on for just one second?" I held my hand over the phone and said to Tina, "Do you mind if I take this call real quick? If you want to take a break, I can come get you when I'm off."

"Oh, yeah, sure."

When the door closed behind Tina, I took my hand off the receiver. "Sorry about that. We're in the middle of getting ready for rush and there's a lot going on here." The receiver slipped in my sweaty hand.

"No problem." She paused. "I got your message. What about this Saturday?"

"Oh, um, I would love to but I'm tied up with sorority rush all weekend. What about next weekend? Are you free next Saturday?"

"Yeah, I could do that."

"Where do you want to go? The only beer place I've really been to off-campus is Blueberry Hill on Delmar."

"There's a cool place called Flannery's Irish Pub about 15 minutes away. I can pick you up."

"Um, great." My knee bounced up and down.

"Awesome! I'll call you next week and we can figure out an exact time."

"Sounds good. Uh, have a good night." I hung up the phone and stared at it. I couldn't believe I was going to have a beer with Professor Schwartz! The thought of being alone with her electrified my body. My foot tapped faster on the floor. I stared at the phone some more, picturing myself sitting next to her in her car, feeling her next to me, her intense eyes focused on me.

Tina and I finished the first 75 or so forms, then called it quits for the night. As we were on our way out, Becky said, "Hey, can you print out the initial ranking of all the girls before you leave? I'd like to see how things are looking so far."

The initial rankings were calculated based on a combination of the hometown votes, GPA, SAT scores, and extracurricular activities. The inkjet printer loudly printed all 347 girls' names, ranked from #1 all the way to #347.

• • •

Our first one-hour rush party had just ended and the 30 rushees were escorted out of our suite. Becky barked orders. "Okay, everyone, we've only got a half hour before the next party, so we need to be efficient. Everyone grab a voting form and give every girl that you met a score."

"After you've voted, you'll have a few minutes for a bathroom break, then we need to get ready for the next group of rushees."

Everyone cast their votes and stuffed them in the ballot box. Becky started passing out sheets of paper with rushee assignments for the next party.

I grabbed the ballot box before the next party started and Tina and I shut ourselves in the office to enter all the votes in the computer. We could tell when the next party started because Thetas broke into singing and clapping as the rushees entered the suite. We repeated this process until all parties were complete and all votes entered in.

We repeated this process for the seven parties on Saturday night. Then the rest of the Thetas went to a lecture hall to wait for us. Now that all the votes were in, I pressed the "rank" button and the computer churned while calculating the rankings and printing them out for the overhead projector.

When we entered the lecture hall, Becky stood at the front of the room where professors usually stood.

"You have the rankings?"

"Yes," I said, and handed her the printouts.

She took the envelope and pulled out the first sheet, which held the girls ranked 1 to 36. She placed it on the overhead projector. Tina and I sat near the front of the room in case we were needed.

Becky looked up at the sea of women with long hair, makeup, and Theta letters. "Okay, everyone. We've got the rankings. We're going to look at them together, then figure out how many women we want to cut after this first round of parties and who we want to invite back for round two."

As she showed each page, there was some quiet talking. "Okay, so we probably need to cut about 50–75 women after this first round of parties." She took the last two pages showing all the names of everyone with rankings #265 or lower and drew a red line below #283.

"Now we're going to discuss who below that line we should invite back and who above the line we think we shouldn't invite back. I have to turn in our final list of who we're inviting to round two parties tonight."

We finally finished around midnight. Exhausted, I knew we would have to do this all over again for three more rounds of parties over the next few weeks, until we had a list of only about 35–40 girls who we would offer bids to.

After seeing this process, part of me felt pride that I had gotten selected, way back in freshman year. The thought still gave me a boost of confidence. But part of me felt icky knowing that some Thetas judged rushees on the basis of superficial qualities like how pretty they were or how they dressed. And I knew that many rushees would be devastated from the rejection.

Seeing the behind the scenes up close gave me pause. I continued to feel torn between the strong bonds I had formed and the fun I had had as part of Theta and some of the realities behind the Greek system. The selection process favored women that fit into the box of a traditionally beautiful, extroverted, feminine straight woman, so being different was something to hide if you wanted to get in. As I was becoming more true to myself and embracing my identity as a gay woman with a more androgynous look, I could no longer pretend to myself that I fit neatly into a sorority.

31

IS THIS A DATE?

January, Senior Year

After getting back from the gym on campus, I jumped in the shower. I could feel the soreness already starting in my biceps and abs. I meticulously shampooed, shaved, and soaped, then brushed my teeth and gargled some Listerine. I then walked in my towel across the hall to my bedroom.

I put on my best pair of jeans from the Gap, a T-shirt, and my favorite plaid flannel button-down. I went back to the bathroom and added gel to slick back my short hair. Checking myself in the mirror, I sprayed a liberal amount of Tommy for Men cologne by Tommy Hilfiger on the back of my neck and my wrists, and grabbed my ChapStick from my nightstand and put it in my pocket. While happy with my androgynous look for my potential date, I would never present myself like this at a sorority event.

I sat on the black leather couch to wait for Erika to pick me up. My watch said 6:47 p.m. My right foot tapped frantically. Jake in the Hat and my other roommate were probably at a Kappa Sig party, since it was Saturday night.

I checked my watch again. 6:52 p.m. The clean scent of my cologne gave me a boost of confidence.

On our dirty beige rug, a large pizza box stood open. One old slice of sausage and pepperoni sat inside, the cheese solidified and hardened on top. Milwaukee's Best beer cans littered the floor and coffee table. Cigarette ashes covered the table, overflowing from the ashtray. I'm not a neat person by nature, but my roommates were disgusting.

I'd been thinking about Erika all week. As Tina and I entered thousands of rushee ratings into the computer database, my mind kept drifting and I had to ask Tina to repeat them. I worried that I might accidentally type in the wrong number and it could mean the difference between a girl getting a bid from Theta or having her hopes shattered.

My watch now read 7:02 p.m. It was pitch black outside. Suddenly, a loud honk pierced my thoughts. I jumped off the couch, opened the front door, and locked it behind me. Jitters propelled me down two flights of stairs. I saw Erika sitting in the driver seat, smiling in my direction.

Erika's compact car was the kind of practical and affordable car I'd grown up with. I opened the passenger side door, my heart racing.

"Hey," I said as I sat on the worn cloth seat.

"Hey! How are you?"

"Pretty good. Glad to be almost done with rush. Next week we give out bids. Then all the pledge activities start."

"How did you end up in a sorority?"

The hot air from the heater felt good. "Well, I joined my freshman year. A friend convinced me to go through rush, and I started going to parties, which I liked. And then I got a bid and I accepted it." I paused for a second, then quickly added, "I thought I was straight when I joined."

I held my breath to see how she would react to my revelation. But Erika just continued to focus on the road ahead as we passed seedy abandoned buildings and dilapidated storefronts. Her body language revealed nothing.

She asked, "How is that? I mean, not being straight in your sorority?"

"It's hard. It's been really hard. I sometimes wonder why I'm still in it. I'm the only gay person and so much of the culture revolves around parties with fraternities. One of my sisters just quit. I sometimes wonder if I should too."

"Okay, here we are." Erika smiled and said, "You ready?" Her smile penetrated to my core.

The area looked rough, like most of the neighborhoods I had been to in St. Louis. As we entered, almost all the tables and barstools were full. "Table for two?" asked the hostess. She sat us at a small table against the wall near the back of the bar and handed us menus.

As I read the extensive list of beers on tap, I saw my menu shaking and tried to steady my hands, so Erika couldn't see. I was too amped up to make eye contact. When the waitress arrived, we both ordered pints of beer.

After ordering, I looked up at Erika. Her eyes locked on mine and I squirmed in my seat. Waitresses scurried back and forth, balancing trays with glasses of beer. My foot tapped uncontrollably under the table. "Um, so how is your dissertation going?"

"It's going okay. I've been collecting a lot of data from my experiments, but some aren't turning out like I thought they would.

And, now that school has started again, I am spending a lot of time teaching, so don't have as much time for my research."

Our waitress arrived at our table holding our pints. The sweet but slightly bitter beer tasted delicious. I hoped it would ease my nerves. We chatted while sipping our beers, finished them quickly and ordered another. Then another.

My foot stopped tapping after the buzz from my second pint kicked in. Erika's smooth voice pulled me in. Whatever activity hummed around us, I didn't notice. I watched her move her finger down the side of the glass before picking it up and taking a sip. She looked into my eyes.

A few moments after the waitress placed our third beers on the table, Erika broke eye contact and looked down at her beer. She looked up again and quietly asked "So, Kristin. Is this a date?"

My brain raced to find the right response. I smiled and replied, "Do you want this to be a date?" I clenched my glass and waited for her response.

Erika fidgeted with her glass, sliding it ever so slightly back and forth across the table. She focused on it, looking lost in thought. Then she looked up and said "I mean, yes. Yes, I do want it to be a date." My heart jumped with excitement. She took a big gulp of beer, then asked, "What do you want? I mean, do you want it to be a date?"

"Yes, I do too." I took a big gulp of beer as well.

Speaking quickly, Erika continued. "So, I've got a question for you. This isn't just some sort of student-teacher crush, is it? I mean, if it is, I'm not interested. Do you always have crushes on your teachers?"

"I've never had a crush on a teacher before." This was true. We both took large gulps of beer and looked at each other, and I said,

"So, can I ask you something?"

"Sure."

"Well, I hope you don't think this is rude, but I've just got to ask. You're gay, right? I mean, I am, but I haven't been able to figure out if you are."

Erika took another gulp of beer and finished it off. "You want another?" She flagged the waitress for two more.

I continued to look at Erika, dying for her answer. She didn't say anything, fidgeted with her empty glass, running her fingers back and forth on the top of the rim.

She said, "Well, I'm a little embarrassed to say, but I'm not sure." She took another sip, looking uncomfortable. I had only seen her confident, charismatic side in the classroom. Seeing her vulnerable side only made me more intensely attracted to her.

"Well, I've never actually been with a woman before." She stared at her beer after saying this and it looked like she was blushing.

"Okay. Do you think you might want to be with a woman?"

She quickly answered "Yes." We both took sips of beer with our eyes locked.

Clearing my throat, I decided to go in a different direction. "How old are you?"

"I'm 29. How old are you?" *Wow, 29. That's hot.*

"22."

After another beer, we left. When I got in her car, I considered how I could prolong the night. I didn't want to go home yet. *What should I say?*

She turned the heater on full blast and started to drive back in the direction of my apartment. My watch said 11:15 p.m. I was not ready for the night to end. I needed to do something quickly. "So, you said you have a dog and a cat?"

"Yes."

"Um, I'd love to come over and meet them." *Did I really just say that? I just said I want to meet her pets.*

Quickly she responded with "Yeah, that sounds great," and made an immediate U-turn. Both of my feet were now tapping uncontrollably on the floor of her car.

We parked outside an old three-story apartment building in a working-class neighborhood. "We're here."

We walked up to the second floor. She fumbled with her keys, opened the door, and flipped on the light. Her little dachshund slid on the worn hardwood floors as he rushed to the door to greet us. Her cat welcomed Erika by rubbing against her leg. "Sorry for the mess."

"No worries. You should see mine. I live with two frat guys. This is clean in comparison." I looked around. In the living room, bookcases overflowing with books lined the walls.

"Let's sit on the couch," Erika said, motioning across the room.

"Okay, that sounds good."

As we sat on the threadbare couch, adrenaline surged through me. *I can't believe I'm sitting here with my professor right now. This is insane!* She sat facing me, just a few inches away.

After a few minutes of conversation, we started to make out. This was not like my first kiss with Sarah at all. These were wet, passionate, strong kisses. She swept me away to a different world. Her hands squeezed my knees, sending shivers up my body. Lost in the moment, we traced the contours of each other's bodies. I was aware of nothing except her touch.

Then she said, "Why don't we go in the bedroom?" I followed her through the dining room and kitchen to the bedroom and her queen-size bed. The lights were off and stayed off.

With no hesitation, our clothes quickly disappeared. My naked skin touched hers. We kissed hard and passionately.

Afterward, we were still and spent. She invited me to stay over and I agreed. Naked, she lay on her back. I put my head on her chest, my arm wrapped tightly around her waist. We snuggled under the soft down comforter. The room began to spin.

I thought to myself, *I can't believe I just had sex with my teacher. I'm lying here naked next to my teacher*! No longer lost in the moment of passion, my intense feelings now began to turn into insecurity. The clock on her bedside table read 2:30 a.m. I remained wide awake. She began to snore softly. I rolled on my back, staring at the ceiling, a little nauseous from the alcohol. I rolled on my side, then my stomach, then my side, then my back. My feelings of being intimidated and in awe of Professor Schwartz resurfaced.

At about 7:30 a.m., when Erika awoke, it felt like I hadn't slept at all. "Want some coffee?" she asked.

"For sure."

She reached into the freezer and pulled out a bag of whole coffee beans. The green packaging had a picture of a mermaid on it. I had only had Folgers out of a can when I lived with my parents or Bears Den house or instant coffee in college. "What kind of coffee is that?"

"It's called Starbucks. I had it while I was in Seattle and get it shipped here. It's very good."

As we sipped the hot coffee from large mugs, we sat at the corner of her kitchen table, which was covered in books. She cleared some space for us and we faced each other, our knees touching.

She had given me a new toothbrush to use, so I felt okay when she kissed me, tasting like creamy coffee. The kiss was long and warm. This was no timid kiss married couples give before going to work. This was the kiss of lovers engaged in an illicit affair. This was what I'd imagined a secret affair would feel like.

After she dropped me off at my apartment, memories of the night before carried me through the day. *I can't believe she had never been with a woman before. I never would've guessed. And I can't believe I just slept with Professor Schwartz! That was the hottest, most intense night of my life!*

32

THUMPER

February, Senior Year

A man twirled and bounced onto the stage, grabbed the microphone, and enthusiastically yelled, "Y'all ready for tonight's show?! We've got a fabulous lineup of the best drag queens in St. Louis! First up is the lovely Miss Cocoa! Give her a warm welcome!"

Erika took my hand as we sipped our bottles of Bud Light. Small circular tables and chairs faced the stage in the small dive bar.

The audience clapped and whooped as Erika's friend Tom sashayed out in a floor-length scarlet dress covered in red sequins. The strapless dress hugged Miss Cocoa like a glove. She walked effortlessly in tall red platforms. Her massive wig consisted of platinum hair piled high, with a few curly strands flowing down. Bright red lipstick, powder-blue eyeshadow, and long fake eyelashes made her shimmer under the spotlight, her mocha skin glowing. Everyone in the audience sang along to "I Will Survive" by Gloria Gaynor—a gay anthem. Miss Cocoa gracefully lip-synched while prancing across the stage with attitude.

We all cheered loudly when the song ended. Miss Cocoa curtseyed, gave a Miss Universe wave, and swished off the stage.

Erika turned to me and asked if she could get me another beer, then kissed me on the lips and said, "I'll be right back."

I watched as gay men and lesbians of all ages filled the bar. A couple of neon signs and colorful lights aimed at the stage gave the bar a warm feeling. Sipping from our glass bottles, we sat with our shoulders touching.

"So, what do you think of the drag show?" Erika asked.

I had never seen one before. "I'm kinda blown away that these guys feel empowered enough to get up on stage dressed as women."

"Yeah, it's great they have a safe space to express themselves like that."

"Yeah. And they're really fun to watch!"

After the show ended, Erika and I stood behind the bar. Tom came out from the back, dressed in sweats and a hoodie. His wig and makeup had vanished.

Erika greeted Tom with, "You were great! Congrats!" She hugged him and planted a big kiss on his cheek.

"Thank you, girl! Did the dress make me look fat?"

"Of course not," Erika said.

I said, "Yeah, you were great up there!"

"Aww, you know how to make a lady blush!"

After saying goodbye to Tom, we drove back to Erika's apartment and I stayed over, as usual.

• • •

A week after we saw the drag show, Erika invited me over for dinner. When I arrived at her place on Friday night, Erika opened the door with a huge grin on her face. "Hi, Thumper." Her nickname for me started when she noticed my nervous habit of tapping my foot. She closed her door, pulled me into her arms, and we made out for a few minutes.

An unfamiliar but delicious spicy smell permeated the air. "What are you making? It smells so good!"

A huge pot sat on the stove and steam seeped out of it. A cutting board and knife sat beside the sink with some large potato chunks resting, mid-cut.

"I'm making my famous Indian orange curried potatoes! I hope you like them."

I'd never eaten Indian food before. "I'm excited to try it."

In Nashville, I'd enjoyed my share of Southern cooking: biscuits, blackberry preserves, corn grits, and salted country ham. In Dallas, I enjoyed Tex-Mex food like steak fajitas and guacamole. If we went out to eat it was either for pizza and pasta at a casual Italian restaurant, or occasionally for Chinese food; won ton soup and beef and snow pea stir fry were my favorites. On my birthday, I often requested Benihana for Japanese.

"I hope you like spicy."

"I love spicy! I grew up on jalapeños and salsa."

Erika took my hand and said, "Come and talk to me in the kitchen while I finish up. I'm almost done and then it just needs to simmer for a while."

As I followed her into the brightly lit kitchen, her dog and cat followed us in. "Thank you so much for cooking for me. It's so sweet. Nobody has ever cooked for me before."

"What, really? Well, I'm glad to be the first." She smiled.

After she finished cutting the last of the potatoes into large chunks, she dropped them into the creamy-looking orange sauce in the pot. The liquid bubbled as she placed the cover back on. "Okay, done for now. Let's go sit on the couch. It should be done in about an hour."

We settled into the couch, my legs draped over her lap and her hands on my legs. Her cat nestled into the chair across the room while her dog curled up in its bed.

Erika began to fiddle with the couch fabric. She looked up and said, "So, I told Dr. Eisenberg about us." Dr. Eisenberg was her dissertation supervisor.

I stared at her in disbelief. "You did? What did he say?"

"Not much really. I had already scoured the student and faculty handbook to make sure there was nothing in there about teachers not being able to date a student. It's not against the rules, as long as the student isn't actively in one of the professor's classes."

"Wow, that must have been hard. So, he didn't really react at all?"

"He looked surprised. At first, I just said I was dating a former student of mine. He didn't have much reaction to that and just said it shouldn't be a big issue, since we didn't get together until after you were out of my class. Then he asked who it was and I told him your name. He looked a bit confused when I said your name and said he didn't know you. It felt really awkward, but then we just started talking about experiments and that was it."

"So, do you feel better about it now that he knows?"

"Yeah. I do. There's a good chance he would have found out anyway, since you're always stopping by my office and we're together on campus a lot. I wanted to tell him before he figured it out. I was worried it might affect our professional relationship, but I think it's going to be okay."

"Well, I'm glad it worked out. Maybe we won't have to try so hard to hide things." I leaned over and kissed her.

After a few moments she reluctantly pulled away and said, "Let me go check on the curry. It's probably almost ready."

She cleared some books and articles off the kitchen table, then filled two cups with water. "You're going to need this."

A minute later she brought over two steaming bowls filled with white rice and orange curry. Cilantro covered the top. I dug in. The creamy curry and soft potatoes melded together perfectly. My mouth filled with heat from the spice immediately after I took a bite.

I took a big gulp of water and said, "This is really hot. What is it made of?"

"The spiciness is from cayenne pepper. The curry sauce has tomato paste, garlic, cream, lemon juice, and some Indian spices. It's also got some yogurt in it to add tanginess. Do you like it?"

"I love it! It's the best thing I've eaten in a long time."

After dinner, we ended up in the bedroom. After steamy sex and simultaneous orgasms, we both fell asleep quickly afterward.

• • •

"I'll take one red carnation," I said.

"$1, please" said the student behind the folding table in the Student Union on the morning of Valentine's Day. I handed over a $1 bill. "Please write the name of the person you want us to deliver it to and their address."

I wrote Erika's name and the address for her office in the

psychology building.

"We're delivering all the flowers by 3 p.m. today."

Despite my excitement, I managed to wait until after 3 to drop by Erika's office. When I peered around the corner, she was reading a book and scribbling something in a notebook. The single red carnation sat in a soda bottle filled with water right next to her. The flower added color to an otherwise neutral space.

"Happy Valentine's Day!" I said.

She looked up and beamed at me. "It was delivered when I was with students during office hours. I was so embarrassed and I know I must've blushed." She paused. "That was so sweet, Thumper. Nobody has ever given me flowers before."

I looked behind me to see that nobody was in the hallway. When I saw the coast was clear, I snuck a quick kiss. "So, how long are you going to be at the lab tonight?"

"I'm not sure. Probably until pretty late. I've got to check on the experiments and finish up some grading. Do you want to come over at nine?"

After leaving Erika's office, I drove to the grocery store to pick something up, then to her apartment. I crawled in through the dog door in the back, like I did when it was late and I didn't want to wake her. Her dog greeted me. I opened the bag of red, pink, white, and silver heart confetti that I had bought and sprinkled it all over her bedspread. Then I placed a Valentine's Day card in the middle. I left her apartment filled with excitement.

When I arrived back at her place at 9 p.m., Erika showered me with kisses and a gift certificate for a 60-minute massage at a place nearby. I had never had a massage before and was intrigued.

• • •

Soon after Valentine's Day, Erika asked me to be her girlfriend. "I love you so much and don't want to date anybody else."

Although completely infatuated with Erika, I felt hesitant. Sarah and I had been off and on during the first semester of this year and hadn't been fully broken up for that long. Erika and I had only been dating for about a month. *Am I ready to be in an exclusive relationship again?* I felt like I loved Erika, but something in the pit of my stomach gave me pause.

Her expression changed from hopeful to concerned as I took longer and longer to answer.

"I love you too." I kissed her.

After we pulled apart, she asked again with a big smile, "So will you officially be my girlfriend?"

I fidgeted and delayed answering. Eventually, I said, "I love you so much, but I'm not 100 percent sure I'm ready to be in an exclusive relationship again. It just makes me nervous."

Her shoulders slumped. My foot tapped quickly as I waited for her response. She said, "I want us to be exclusive. I wouldn't be able to handle it if you were with anyone else."

I tried to reason with her. "I really want to be with you, but I just don't feel ready to be in an exclusive relationship yet. It's not that I'm dating anyone else or that I necessarily want to, but being exclusive makes me uncomfortable. I don't feel ready. Can we just date for now and decide later?"

"If we're not exclusive, I don't want to date at all. I don't want to just date casually. I can't."

A pit settled in my stomach. I couldn't bear the thought of her breaking up with me, but the thought of being in an exclusive relationship didn't feel right either. I sat motionless, not sure how to respond.

After an uncomfortable silence, she said, "I'm sorry. I just can't date you unless we're exclusive."

I stared at her, then at my lap. I felt like I could hear the ticking of my watch while I considered how to respond. "Can I think about it?"

Her arms were folded across her chest. "Fine, I guess so."

33

THE CATHOLIC GIRL

March, Senior Year

After our favorite gay dance club in St. Louis closed at 1:30 a.m., Barrett, Matt, Kim, and I crossed the bridge over the Mississippi River to East St. Louis, on the Illinois side. We passed abandoned buildings, shady characters engaged in drug deals, and homeless encampments, and parked in front of Faces nightclub on Fourth Street.

I scanned the lot to make sure it looked safe to get out. I often heard about robberies and shootings in St. Louis, but we all knew that East St. Louis was at least ten times worse. Nobody else was in sight. We hustled up to the nondescript black door of a decrepit-looking brick building. A small white sign over the door said FACES in red block letters.

As we entered the massive gay club, music pounded, making the floor vibrate. Gay men in tight shirts with their muscles bulging out and women flaunting cleavage or rocking short, boyish haircuts filled the expansive main floor. The crowd moved provocatively on the huge dance floor. Scattered people smoked cigarettes while they watched the dancers or chatted with friends.

To the left of the club entrance, a bouncer guarded a door that led downstairs to the basement. I had once tried to go down there, but the bouncer said, "No women allowed."

"What's down there?" I asked Matt and Barrett.

Barrett said, "It's basically a cruise bar. There are a bunch of screens playing porn and couches where you can hang out. And there's a back room that's pretty much pitch black where people have sex."

Intrigued, I tried sneaking down there when I saw the door wasn't guarded. I hoped my boyish clothes and short hair might lead people to mistake me for a guy, but no luck. When I got to the bottom of the stairwell a guard asked me to leave, but not before I saw a smoky dark room with porn playing on screens.

We grabbed drinks at the bar, then headed to the packed dance floor. A disco ball rotated above our heads and colored lights ricocheted onto the crowd. Drunk after at least five beers so far that night, I bounced to the music. Kim, who looked exactly like Liza Minnelli with her short dark hair and big innocent-looking eyes, smiled at me.

Earlier that day, when I asked Erika if she wanted to come out with us, she said "No, that's okay. You guys go have fun. I'll see you when you get back." At the moment, I felt relieved.

A few weeks before, Erika had come out with my GLBA friends and me to the gay clubs, for the first time. Probe, also called the Complex, was the biggest and most popular gay bar in St. Louis and we frequented it often. Before settling in to dance, Erika, Barrett, Matt, myself, and a few other friends from GLBA did a walk-through of all the bars and the outdoor area with sand and a volleyball net. After grabbing drinks, we all hit the dance floor.

Erika wore tight, light-washed Gap jeans and a gray long-sleeve shirt that looked like a long john top. She wore no makeup or jewelry. Her stiff, awkward shuffling contrasted with the flamboyant hip-shaking surrounding her. She smiled at me. I had absorbed the dance style of the energetic gay boys that I spent so much time dancing around. We danced facing each other, but not touching.

Barrett wore his typical blue and red button-down tucked into his jeans with a braided brown leather belt. His neatly combed hair and brown topsiders completed his preppy look. He leaned over and yelled, "Check out that guy over there with the tight blue shirt on. I'm gonna go over and talk to him. Wish me luck."

"Good luck!" I expected I wouldn't see Barrett for the rest of the night. He would probably go home with the guy and I'd hear about it tomorrow.

After dancing for a bit, Erika asked if I wanted another beer. I breathed in the spicy citrus of the Joop perfume I had bought her a few weeks before.

After she left, I scanned the dance floor. Women in tight tank tops and heels swirled all around us, their seductive dance moves capturing my attention. *I shouldn't be looking at other women. What am I doing?* I tried to tear my gaze away, but found it difficult.

Erika came back and handed me another beer, resuming her awkward shuffling. The fake smile on her face told me what I already knew: she wasn't having a good time. She had told me she didn't like to go out and dance, but I had convinced her to come.

After we had only been there for about an hour, she told me she was ready to go anytime. My heart sank. "It's still really early. It's only midnight."

"Yeah, well, I'm kinda tired and I've got a lot of work I need to do in the morning, so I don't want to stay out too late."

"Oh, okay. Let me just say goodbye."

When we got back to her apartment, she fell asleep quickly. I lay awake, wishing I were still out dancing with my friends. An empty and distant feeling washed over me. That was the last time Erika ever went out dancing with me.

• • •

Back at Faces, Matt leaned in and yelled to Barrett, Kim, and me, "It's almost midnight. Let's go upstairs and get a good seat for the show." The four of us walked upstairs and found seats in front of the large stage. The seats quickly filled up. Behind me I heard "Jell-O shot? $2."

Barrett said, "I'll take four!" He handed a $10 bill to the drag queen holding a tray of dozens of little plastic cups filled with red, yellow, orange, green, and blue Jell-O shots. "Keep the change."

He then looked at us and said, "Come on guys, pick one!"

I selected an orange shot.

"Alright, on the count of three! One, two, three!" We all tipped our heads back with our Jell-O shots simultaneously. The liquor filled my chest and I swallowed it whole.

A few minutes later, the first drag queen pranced out, greeted by loud clapping and whistling. She began to lip-sync, sashaying around the stage as everyone sang along, cheering for every head snap and hip thrust.

Kim sat to my right. A sophomore, she had just started attending GLBA meetings this year and had started coming out to clubs with us recently. Sometimes we studied together in the Catholic Student

Center across from campus, where she was a member. They offered big tables and a quiet space. She studied her mechanical engineering textbooks and spoke of her dreams to work at NASA, while I pored over psychology books and spoke of the case files of schizophrenic and bipolar patients that I read at my part-time job.

Barrett and Kim hung out all the time. He said she had never been with a woman and had a major crush on me. I could tell. She hung on my every word and would always make an effort to sit or stand by me, talk to me, and laugh at my stories. I found her innocence and puppy dog eyes charming.

After the drag show, we all hit the dance floor again, dirty dancing with each other.

Kim and I moved over to the bar to take a break and order more beer. She looked at me intently and seemed to sway a little. Our bodies almost touched, we were so close. She touched my arm and said, "You know, I think you're really cute." She smiled broadly, then looked down at the floor.

I couldn't help but smile back. At this point I still had doubts about whether girls would find me attractive. I'd only been with two women and nobody had ever hit on me before. With guys I'd had a long history and I knew there was something about me they liked; I had some semblance of self-confidence with them. With women I had zilch—so it didn't take much more than a good personality, alcohol, and a little flattery to make me feel attracted to Kim.

After a few moments, I said, "I have to say, you're pretty cute yourself."

She looked like she was blushing as she stroked her beer lightly with her fingers and looked down. Then she said, "You know, I've never kissed a girl before."

As soon as she said it, all I could think about were her lips, and what it would be like to kiss her. I tried to shake the thoughts from my head and took another sip of beer. Our faces were just inches away, her hopeful eyes staring right into mine.

Suddenly, hot passionate kisses swept us up in the moment. After some making out, a slap of guilt pulled me away from her. I blurted out, "I'm so sorry. I shouldn't be doing this. I have a girlfriend." My cloudy head made me unsteady.

Looking disappointed, she said "Oh, okay."

I stepped away from her and said, "It's not that I didn't enjoy it. Um, I did. But I just can't."

"Yeah, I understand." Kim looked down at the floor again, shoulders slumped.

My mind reeled. A stab of guilt pierced my stomach. *I can't believe I just did that!* A wave of nausea overtook me. I chugged more beer.

"I'll be back. I'm gonna go the bathroom." I felt vomit welling up in my throat, and leaned over the toilet, but didn't throw up. A couple of tears trickled down my face as I stood in the stall. *What is wrong with me? Now I've ruined everything.* I thought back to a few weeks prior. After a few days of stress over Erika's ultimatum, I had agreed to be exclusive. *I'm such an idiot.*

A blur of torment haunted me the rest of the night. I avoided Kim while simultaneously feeling drawn to her as I watched her dance. I continued to feel a breath away from throwing up.

As Barrett drove us home, a terrible feeling of dread overwhelmed me as I thought of seeing Erika that night. "Can you drop me off at home instead of at Erika's?" I often stopped by her place after going clubbing, but I couldn't face her that night.

When I got home, I chugged a few glasses of water in the kitchen, then swallowed three ibuprofen. I changed into boxers and a T-shirt and collapsed in bed, but I lay there unable to fall asleep, replaying the kiss over and over in my head. But then darkness swept through my body as I imagined Erika sleeping peacefully in her apartment, unaware of what I had done. Dizziness overcame me when I tried to close my eyes. The room started to spin from all the alcohol, so I sat up in bed.

I leaned into my hands and cried. And cried. At some point I managed to pass out from exhaustion. I slept fitfully through the night, getting up to pee a couple of times. I kept picturing Erika's reaction. I imagined her yelling at me, crying, and breaking up with me. After a few minutes thinking about this, I would fall back asleep, only to wake up again a few hours later.

I was drowning in a tsunami of guilt. *Will Erika be angry and break up with me? Will she be hurt and cry?* Both possibilities made my head pound harder. I rolled back and forth in bed, trying to get comfortable, but couldn't.

I sat up in bed, then eventually managed to drag myself out of it. I grabbed my backpack and stuffed a few textbooks and notebooks in, then put my jacket on, grabbed my keys, and left. On the drive to campus, I couldn't shake thoughts of my drunken kiss with Kim. *I can't believe I did that. I don't even like her in that way. I'm such an idiot. Now I've screwed everything up.*

I bought a croissant and a large coffee from the Student Union and ate as I walked to the library. I walked up one flight of stairs and found a spot at a long table; not many students were studying on a Sunday morning.

After reading a few pages, my mind wandered back to Erika and Kim. I tried to pull my focus back to my book. After a few hours of minimal productivity, I packed up. On the way out, emotion again overtook me. I fought back tears.

Long afternoon shadows from trees covered the path. I managed to keep my tears in until I got to my car. Then I sobbed.

Okay, I know I just have to do it—I have to tell her. I hope she doesn't break up with me. I'm so in love with her. I wiped the tears from my eyes, then drove slowly to Erika's apartment.

Erika opened the door with a wide smile and took me in her arms and kissed me. Her dog jumped up and down. I pulled back and said, "There's something I have to talk to you about."

Her brow furrowed in concern and she said, "Oh, okay. Come in. Are you alright?" She walked over to the armchair closest to the door and sat down.

I stood awkwardly in front of her, my hands stuffed in my pockets. She leaned forward in the chair with her hands on her knees. I heard her cat meow somewhere behind me.

I looked into her expectant eyes. I felt like crying again.

She eventually said "What is it? You've got me worried."

I looked into her eyes and saw a trusting woman who loved me deeply. She had recently come home to Austin with me over spring break and met my parents, who were now very accepting of me being gay. They loved how intelligent and articulate she was. My mom and her seemed to bond over their vast vocabularies and passion for science.

I quickly blurted out, "Something happened last night." I took a deep breath and stuffed my hands further into the pockets of my jeans. "We were at Faces, and I got really drunk, and Kim and I kissed." I looked at the floor and clenched my hands together.

Erika didn't say anything at first. After a few moments of silence,

I looked up. She looked shocked.

I continued, "I am so, so sorry. I don't know what happened. I was really drunk and I just wasn't thinking. I'm so sorry and I love you. I'm so sorry. I'm just so sorry." Tears began to drip down my face as I looked at her long lashes and intense eyes.

"Why would you do this? Do you like her?" She crossed her arms.

"I was just really, really drunk and she has a crush on me and made a move. I don't even like her like that at all. I love you and I won't do it again. I'm so sorry. I'm such an idiot." I got down on my knees in front of her and cried.

"Do you still want to be with me? Or do you want to date her?" Tears started to drip down her cheeks too.

I looked up at her, my face wet with tears. "I want to be with you. I love you so much. I don't want to be with her at all. I'm so sorry. I was just drunk."

She looked at me intensely. I looked back at her and waited. The quiet of the room was only broken by the sound of occasional cars passing by. I continued to kneel in front of her.

"What you did really hurts me, but I love you too." She paused. "I forgive you. Just promise me you will never do it again."

I placed my hands in her hands, moist from crying. We squeezed them tightly together.

"I'm so sorry I hurt you. I love you so much and I don't want to lose you. I feel so awful for what I did and wish I could take it back."

Erika started to cry again. I got up and hugged her. We both cried while locked in a long embrace.

Eventually, exhausted, we slowly pulled away. I moved forward for a kiss and she kissed me back passionately. I could taste the salt from our tears on her lips.

• • •

I wish I could say that our relationship was smooth sailing after this, but it wasn't. This was not the last time I cheated on Erika with Kim. It was only the first.

About a half-dozen other times, I repeated the same pattern. Erika didn't come out dancing with my friends and me. I got drunk, Kim got drunk, Kim and I kissed, and on one occasion had sex. I apologized to Erika. I cried. She cried. We made up. I promised not to do it again. Then, I did it again. And again.

I knew I had issues with alcohol. That's when I always did things I later regretted. Since freshman year, a few people had told me I had a drinking problem, but I tried to shrug it off like they were just uptight. At first, I told myself I just liked to party and have fun and it was no big deal. Later, I tried cutting down many weekends, but never managed to. I tried to just have a few drinks, but usually ended up getting drunk. I didn't know any women that drank more than me, so it was hard to keep kidding myself that I didn't have a problem. I went to a couple of AA meetings in Jackson Hole, the summer I worked there after freshman year, but didn't continue once I got back to school. I spoke to my psychologist about it on many occasions. Alcohol combated my natural shyness and self-consciousness, and I often didn't feel confident enough to navigate social situations without it.

I didn't stop drinking and a couple months later, in a heart-wrenching conversation, I broke up with Erika. I cried many nights afterward. Kim and I never dated.

34

LAVALIER

April, Senior Year

Barrett and I sat on the edge of a king-size bed in one of my sorority sisters' rooms in a posh hotel. He leaned in and whispered to me, "You know what would be funny? If we kissed, just to freak people out!"

Dozens of couples milled about the suite with beer bottles or cocktails in plastic cups. Tuxes and sparkly ballgowns packed the room, different perfumes and colognes mixing with the smell of alcohol. Lively chatting enveloped the pre-party. Barrett and I both sipped Jack Daniels whiskey and coke.

I said, "Yeah, we should totally do it. That would freak out and confuse people." By now everyone in my sorority knew I was gay, since I had come out in the student newspaper.

Barrett raised his eyebrows and said, "Okay, let's do it!"

We looked around. Most people were engaged in conversations or focused on their drinks. Barrett wore a classic black-and-white tuxedo. He had fashion sense enough to avoid a ruffled shirt or a baby blue jacket, unlike some of the other guys.

We leaned in and started to kiss, adding in a little tongue to make it more realistic. It lasted a moderate amount of time—not a peck you give your grandmother, but also not a full sucking-face session. Like a kiss with a straight boy, but less sloppy. *This must be what it's like for actors to kiss someone on camera.* Slightly awkward, but not awful.

We stopped, then slowly looked around to assess the reactions. I was hoping for eyes bulging out and eyebrows raised—and there were a few—but most people hadn't even noticed. We looked at each other and attempted to stifle our laughs. Unable to hold it in, we both started cracking up.

Barrett whispered, "Maybe we should do it again."

"Okay, why not."

We kissed again and saw a few confused looks. We couldn't help from cracking up again.

"Do you want to get another drink or go down to the party?" I asked him.

"Let's go down. I'm kind of hungry."

"Yeah, me too. Plus, this is getting kind of boring and I'm ready to dance!"

We took the elevator down to the first floor and followed a few others in formal wear to a massive ballroom. We walked straight over to the buffet and grabbed plates. I motioned to a large round table about half full. "Let's go sit over there."

One of my roommates from the year before sat at the table with her date. I introduced Barrett and she introduced us to her date. As we ate, I noticed Andrea, a Theta sister, across the table wearing her new necklace, fresh from her announcement during our last chapter meeting.

Toward the end of the meeting, our President had gotten up and said, "Okay everyone, we've got a very special announcement tonight. Everyone gather around in a big circle."

We formed a huge circle of about 100 women, stretching from the bottom of the lecture hall where the chalkboards were, up the aisles on both sides, and all the way across one of the rows of seats. After everyone was settled, someone turned off the lights. We stood in the dark. As my eyes started to adjust, I saw our president holding a single tall white candle. She lit it with a lighter, then looked around the circle and said, "Okay, everyone ready to sing? On one...two...three."

Everyone started singing the special song for this ceremony: words of love, sweet and slow. Our president passed the candle slowly to the left, from one girl to the next, around the circle. When the candle reached each girl, everyone watched intensely to see if she would blow it out.

When the candle reached Rebecca, it sounded like people held their breath. She had been dating Shawn, a Theta Xi, for almost a year. Rebecca held the candle in her hand, looked at it, then slowly passed it to the girl on her left. I heard a collective sigh.

We continued to sing the same song repeatedly as my sisters passed the candle around the circle. It got closer to me, only a few people away now. My sister to the right slowly passed me the candle and I took it. The heat radiating from it warmed my face. I looked at the glowing flame and knew that nobody would think I would blow it out. I quickly passed it along.

As the orange flame had nearly been passed all the way around the circle, I wondered if it would go past the president for a second round. If it did, that meant someone had gotten engaged. The room collectively held their breath again as the flame closed in on the president. The candle had now burned one third of the way down. Wax dripped onto the candle holder. Before getting to the president, the candle stopped at Andrea. She held it for a moment, then quickly inhaled and blew out the candle.

Everyone started clapping and cheering, filling the room with high-pitched squeals of delight. I clapped weakly. All the lights flipped on, momentarily blinding us. Everyone started chanting, "Story, story, story, story!" Andrea grinned from ear to ear.

The room started to quiet down until only the tick of the huge clock in the front of the room could be heard. The whole room gazed at Andrea in anticipation and envy. I thought to myself, *I hope this doesn't take too long. I really have to pee.*

Andrea couldn't hide her joy. "Well, most of you know that my boyfriend Dave and I have been together about six months. We met at our mixer with Sig Ep. Anyway, this past Friday night he took me to dinner at an Italian restaurant. It was super romantic. When we got back, he said he had a surprise for me."

Everyone leaned in further, so as not to miss a single word.

Andrea continued. "He took me to the exact spot in the Sig Ep house where we met and got down on one knee, then took out a little red velvet jewelry box and opened it. He took out the gold fraternity lavalier with the ΣAE letters on it and a gold chain and said 'Andrea, I love you so much. Will you accept my lavalier?' I couldn't believe it! I was so surprised! I cried as he put the lavalier around my neck."

I watched as everyone cheered and rushed over to hug Andrea. Through the crowd I could see everyone fawn over the necklace. Andrea held it up, then one of the girls put it on for her. As she basked in the glory and envy, I hung back.

Behind the cheers, I know what most of the girls were thinking, because I had heard them talking about it to each other. "My boyfriend sucks. We've been together for more than a year and he still hasn't lavaliered me." "I can't wait for my boyfriend to propose to me! I wonder how he's going to do it? He better do it soon—we've been together more than two years!"

I felt like an alien from outer space watching some strange human ritual. I had stood through many of these lavalier ceremonies, unique to Greek culture, over the course of my four years in the sorority and always felt like an outsider. I started to imagine what it would have been like if I had been so in love with Sarah that I wanted to affirm or celebrate our relationship during the ceremony, like everyone else. What would I even do? Would I give her my sorority letters on a necklace to her as a promise to seal our relationship like straight couples do? *Okay, first off I doubted she would want to wear my sorority letters—she wasn't Theta's biggest fan.*

In my mind, I imagined that I had just given Sarah a promise "necklace" that didn't have my sorority letters and she accepted. Now I wanted to celebrate this in the candle ceremony. Here is how I imagined things going.

The candle is passed around and I blow out the candle. Everyone yells, "Story! Story! Story!"

"Well, most of you know that my girlfriend Sarah and I have been together about six months. Anyway, this past Friday night I took her to dinner at an Italian restaurant off campus. It was super romantic. When we got to campus, I said I had a surprise for her. I took her to the exact spot on campus where we met—in a basement, at a GLBA meeting—and got down on one knee. I took out a little red velvet jewelry box and opened it, took out a gold necklace, and said 'Sarah, I love you so much. Will you accept this promise necklace?' She said yes and I put it around her neck!"

I imagined the jaws dropping, the confused looks, the silence, the avoidance, the angry looks, and the lack of excitement and envy—I had already experienced these reactions, slow dancing with Sarah and coming out in my sorority. I imagined the thoughts going through their heads. *Who is she to think her relationship is like one between a man and a woman? The ceremony is sacred and it isn't for her. Kristin must be confused. Maybe I should talk to her about finding the Lord and getting on the right path.* There would be no cheering, maybe just a few awkward claps. There might be a couple of genuine hugs, but mostly strained, weak hugs or none at all.

I shook these thoughts from my mind and focused in again on the swarm of girls surrounding Andrea. I walked over to where my backpack sat underneath a desk, grabbed it, changed out of my robe into regular clothes, and snuck out of the lecture hall without talking to anyone.

At formal, Andrea displayed her gold lavalier necklace prominently in her cleavage. Dave sat next to her with his arm around her.

After Barrett and I finished eating, we hit the dance floor, weaving through the crowd to the center. We danced vigorously to a few songs, then Barrett leaned in. "There are some totally cute guys here. All-American, just my type. Too bad they're all straight!"

After about an hour of dancing with Barrett, I suggested we get out of there and go to Probe. "I've got to get out of these clothes. They're driving me crazy!"

We both changed into jeans and a button-down, then packed our formal-wear in garment bags.

Anticipation moved through my veins as we entered Probe. Clubgoers wore tight jeans and tight shirts, but moved freely to the music. The dance floor was not filled with guys who looked like they were wearing their dad's suit, shuffling their feet back and forth, wishing they weren't dancing. There were no prim and proper girls in satin dresses and pearl necklaces. Clothes were edgy and revealing. The atmosphere was eclectic and sexy and dark instead of shiny and preppy.

We joined our GLBA friends on the dance floor and were greeted with warm hugs and huge smiles. The pounding club beats echoed inside me. I felt like I could be completely myself here—short hair, androgynous clothes, men's cologne, and all. The five of us danced with abandon until the club closed.

35

PFLAG

End of Second Semester, Senior Year

I sat in a folding chair in a large community space in St. Louis. A lady with graying hair standing at the podium said, "We've got a special treat tonight. A student from the Washington University gay and lesbian organization is going to speak to us about her coming-out experiences. Please give a warm welcome to Kristin Griffith!"

The crowd of more than 100 people clapped. Most sat in folding chairs, but a few stood in the back. I tried breathing deeply, hoping to soften my nerves—with no luck.

PFLAG (Parents and Friends of Lesbians and Gays) had recently contacted the GLBA about having a student speak at their weekly meeting. As the new GLBA president, I volunteered. PFLAG is a national nonprofit organization with over 200,000 members and supporters in the United States. Its goal is to promote the health and well-being of parents, families, and friends of gay, lesbian, bisexual, and transgender individuals. It was founded in 1972 when Jeanne Manford marched with her gay son in a New York pride parade. After many gay and lesbian people ran up to Jeanne during the parade and begged her to talk to their parents, she decided to start a support group.

I walked toward the front of the expansive hall, the wood floors creaking beneath my feet, the mustiness of the old building filling my nose. Once I got up to the front, I placed my notes, slightly crumpled, on the weathered wooden podium.

I took a deep breath and looked out at the crowd. I saw parents' weathered, sad faces, and worried eyes. I saw men with hands stuck in their pockets, standing in the back. All eyes were glued on me. The room was so quiet I could have heard a mouse run across it. All I heard was the *thump, thump, thump* of my heart in my ears.

"Um, hi everyone. I'm Kristin. I'm a senior at Washington University. I'm a psychology major. And…I came out as gay last year."

Thump, thump, thump. I glanced at my notes. *What does that say?*

Everyone waited with interest. "So, uh, where to start."

The woman who had introduced me smiled and nodded.

I started again. "Okay, so, when I started college I thought I was straight. I dated guys in high school and never had any clue that I might be gay. I grew up in Dallas and in Nashville and I had never met anyone gay before. I thought of it as something really awful that you didn't want to be. And my family wasn't religious, but I'd heard people say that gay people go to Hell. Anyway, I dated a lot in high school, and I thought guys were fine."

Hundreds of eyes peered at me curiously. I stopped clenching my notes and started gesturing with my hands as I talked, like I normally do.

"Everything changed for me at the beginning of my sophomore year. My ex-boyfriend from freshman year came out to me as gay.

He was the first gay person I had ever met. Once he came out to me, I started to freak out—I started to worry that I might be gay too. I started to think about my feelings about women and realized I'd had crushes on women, but didn't realize that's what they were at the time. At first, I thought I might be bisexual just like my ex thought he was at first, but over time I eventually figured out I was a lesbian."

"The last thing I wanted was to be gay. So, I basically spent my entire sophomore year continuing to hook up with and casually date guys. I tried really hard to be straight. I mean, no one can say I didn't try. I always broke up with guys for no reason in particular. I'd had guys cry over me when I broke up with them, but I had never once cried over a guy. And I just didn't understand when my sorority sisters would fawn over guys so much. That is, until my first relationship with a girl. Then I finally got it."

"I cried a lot that year and was stressed out a lot. I went to a therapist on campus. And, when I finally told my parents I thought I might be gay they basically told me not to do anything I would regret and that I would need to worry about getting AIDS. They worried about me because they knew my life would be so hard if I was gay. I spent that year feeling very alone and scared."

"Anyway, by the beginning of junior year I met a girl and fell in love with her. She was the first woman I ever kissed, and we became girlfriends. But, I spent most of the year lying to all my friends and sorority sisters and pretending to be straight. It was horrible. I was so excited to have feelings for someone like I'd never had before, but I was scared I would lose my friends if I told them. My sophomore and junior years were the two most stressful years of my life."

"I did end up coming out in my sorority and while most of my sisters were accepting, some sisters who I thought were my friends started to avoid me. I'm still in my sorority, but have found that I spend less and less time there and much more time with my new friends in GLBA. I feel like I can be myself in GLBA and the group really saved me. My sorority revolves so much around dating guys and fraternity-sorority mixers and it just isn't as fun anymore. And I just don't feel like I can truly be myself or like I really belong there. I'm now 100 percent out on campus and it feels so much better."

Looks of concern started to get replaced with looks of hope. After it was over and we were milling about, a woman who looked about 50 came up to me and said, "I really enjoyed hearing you speak. You look very much like my daughter. And it is so nice to hear your story and that you found happiness with a girlfriend, have friends, are doing well in school, and you seem pretty happy."

She started to cry. After a few moments she regained control and continued. "I just worry so much about my daughter...about whether she'll find happiness. I worry that people will always be cruel to her. I worry that people will discriminate against her and she won't be able to get a job. And, I'm still trying to get over the fact that I was taught that gay people will go to Hell. I want to think this isn't the case, but I just don't know."

Tears clung to her eyelashes. She wiped her face with her sleeve.

I said, "I'm really sorry. I know you must worry about your daughter and it's true that it is hard to be gay, because of how society views it. But I don't believe I am going to Hell—well, I don't really believe in Heaven or Hell, but even if I did, I don't think gay people are going to Hell. I took a class on the Psychology of Homosexuality and we studied the passages in the Bible that people often quote as proof that being gay is a sin. We learned that that isn't really what the Bible passages are about."

Dozens of others milled about the community room we stood in. The lighting was warm and bright and voices filled the air. The woman moved in a little closer and spoke again.

"Thank you for saying that. Just being here and speaking to us helps. We're all just struggling to understand and accept this." She moved half a step closer and continued. "You know, my daughter is just so sweet and loving and I just want to protect her. And then sometimes I feel ashamed that she's gay. I feel so guilty that I don't want to tell any of my family and friends, like I did something wrong in raising her. Maybe I wasn't a good enough mother. I'm just having such a hard time with it all."

She wiped another tear from her face. "I just wanted you to know how much I appreciate you sharing your story with us. To know that you have found happiness makes me feel like things could turn out okay for my daughter and me." She stopped and looked into my eyes.

I told her, "I know it's hard now, but it will be okay. It's great that you're coming to these meetings and I know your daughter will appreciate your support. It's been difficult for me, but support from friends and my parents—who ended up coming around pretty quickly—has made all the difference. It takes time, but it will get better."

She moved in and gave me a tight hug, squeezing hard; it felt like the warm hugs from my mom. When she let go, I could see the pain in her eyes, but I was able to keep myself composed as sadness swirled through me. I imagined this was how my mom might have felt.

36

SENIOR SEND-OFF

April, Senior Year

On April 30, 1995, I walked into an expansive hall on campus. White folding chairs surrounded about 15 large circular tables. Black and yellow pansies filled several white vases on each table. White tablecloths, white linen napkins, white plates, real silverware, and fancy glasses sat neatly on the tables.

My sorority sisters filled about two thirds of the chairs. Skirts, dresses, and delicate blouses in pastel colors gave the room a warm glow. The early afternoon sun streamed in through the windows. Heels clicked on the hardwood floors and the fresh scent of shampoo and floral accents of perfume floated in the air.

I found Daniela and joined her. Women hugged and chatted as the room quickly filled up. One of the Theta officers stood and asked us to take a seat. Women settled around the room and their voices began to die down. A few other officers started to pass out Theta song lyrics. Once everyone had them in hand, the officer said, "Okay, Thetas, on the count of three. One, two, three."

Beautiful voices singing words of friendship carried through the air. I sang softly, so people couldn't hear that I couldn't hit the high notes. Once we got to the chorus, the voices seemed to get louder.

As I listened to the song, I could almost still feel the excitement and promise of sorority initiation a little over three years ago. Our whole pledge class had spent more than a month studying Theta history, learning all the chapter rules and commitments, getting to know the 75 women already in Theta, and being wooed by our pledge moms.

As an official Theta after initiation, my pledge mom picked my official Greek name which means strength and courage. The majority of the names selected for the other pledges meant caring, selfless, compassionate, sweet, and other traditionally feminine words. Thinking of my Greek name infused me with a sense of pride. I always loved my name because it was different, and strong and courageous were things I aspired to be.

I remembered back to the comforting routine of our chapter meetings every Sunday night, where we discussed upcoming date parties, charity events, and intramural sports. Freshman year, the older Thetas gave me a yellow and black Theta powder puff football jersey that had CRUNCHY WOMAN printed on the back. I smiled, thinking back to the nickname I cherished—unlike the derogatory names I had been called in my youth.

One of the other officers was giving another goodbye speech. She finished and everyone started snapping. I joined in and looked over at Daniela. She smiled and I smiled back.

Looking around the room, a few of the girls triggered a punch in my gut. A dark cloud washed away the warm feelings I had just experienced. Memories of my sophomore and junior years flooded my brain—all the times I got drunk and forced myself to hook up with yet another guy, so I could try to convince myself I could be straight. All the functions I brought guys to, all the while knowing in my heart that I was only going through the motions to keep up appearances. I lived in constant fear of losing the acceptance and friendship of my sisters—so I lied and pretended to be someone I wasn't. Among my sisters I would talk about the guy I just hooked up with—eliciting excitement from them. Then I would go back to my dorm room and cry.

I wrote in my journal during that time, "I'm sick of being chained in by what I think people want me to be. I'm sick of acting like what people expect. I'm sick of pretending. I'm sick of repressing what I like because of the fear of not being liked. I'm fucking sick of it all."

I remembered the times when a sister made fun of someone by calling her a "lesbo"—while I was in a secret relationship with Sarah. The disgusted stares and angry eyes on Sarah and me as we slow danced at the pajama party. How, after that, some of my sisters seemed to avoid me or only offered an obligatory "hi" when I passed them. They no longer hugged me like they used to.

A conflicting mixture of closeness and distance overwhelmed my thoughts. I shifted uncomfortably in my seat.

Near the closing of the send-off ceremony, one of the officers handed me two letters. I took them, but couldn't look at them right away. Other seniors immediately began reading. I could see someone wiping tears from her eyes with her linen napkin. I heard someone sniffle.

I looked at the first letter, which was from my pledge daughter. I took a breath and started reading.

Dear Kristin,

It feels so weird to write this letter because it's hard to believe you're actually leaving. It feels like I've known you forever (well 3 years isn't forever, but at WU it's a long time). I've known you even longer than I've known Dave! So it feels a little strange that you're actually going to move on with your life.

Even though we're not the type that goes out together on weekends, I've always been proud to call you my mom. From the moment I pledged Theta, you always made me feel comfortable and at home. During mom week, I knew my mom had to be cool, because I got all the coolest toys! And as the years passed, I became more and more proud of you for both what you've done inside Theta and what you've accomplished outside as well.

I know you're a great student and you are very active in other groups, but I'm most proud of what you've done in Theta—to be open about your sexuality. That took more guts than I ever had, but you've been so calm and cool about it. To tell your sisters, not knowing what their reaction would be, shows just how true and strong you really are. I really am going to miss you. I wish you the very best in all you do in the future!

Θ love and mine, Tami

As I read it, I fought back tears. When I finished, I sat staring at it. *I can't believe she thought I was calm and cool about coming out. I never felt calm or cool—I always felt the complete opposite.*

I took a few deep breaths to try to slow my breathing. Next, I picked up the other letter. It was from my parents and written in my mom's handwriting on colorful stationary. I began to read.

Spring 1995

Dear Kristin,

On this special occasion that you are sharing with your friends in Kappa Alpha Theta, we want you to know that we are extremely proud of you. We are proud of you for your achievements—and they are many, both academic and personal—but most of all, we are proud of you because of your many fine qualities of character.

I think that the hardest part of parenting is seeing the pain that a beloved child must experience while growing up. We would have shielded you from that pain, if possible, but perhaps you would not have developed your strength of character, your fortitude, your persistence, your sunny disposition, and all of the other fine qualities that we love and admire in you. You always have been able to cope with the adversity in your life, as well as to celebrate the joyous times to cheer those around you.

As you commence the next phase of your life, the years beyond your life at Washington University, we know that you will always be true to yourself, no matter how difficult that may be at times. We love you very much and support you in your endeavors. We hope that you will want us to share your life as we have always been grateful that you have shared ours.

Love always,
Mommy and Daddy

Although many others in the room now openly wiped tears from their face, I fought back my own overwhelming emotion. I sat rereading Tami and my parents' words. Despite my efforts to stuff my emotions, a single tear dripped down my face. *They are proud of me?* Another tear dripped down.

As I looked around the room, feelings of deep friendship and support from many of my sisters infused the room. I felt this warmth even as many of the pressures of trying to fit into such a straight environment stifled my self-expression with a gray cloud. I wished things were black and white, but they never were.

I walked out of the senior send-off knowing my days at Wash U were numbered. I noticed the mostly dormant trees were now sprouting a few green leaves here and there. Flowers began to peek their way up in gardens that had been empty for months.

EPILOGUE: NEW YEAR'S EVE

December 31, 1997

Two and a half years after I graduated from Wash U, Zoey and I escaped the frigid St. Louis winds and entered a modest apartment for a New Year's Eve party. The heat inside defrosted my bones. I had been close friends with Zoey, a graduate student in art therapy and a lesbian, since my senior year. We had danced many nights away at Attitudes, the most popular lesbian club in St. Louis, and supported each other through intense relationships as well as horrible breakups.

After graduation from Wash U, I had spent two years in St. Louis working as a research assistant at the Washington University School of Medicine. I had just flown back to St. Louis from Houston, where I was attending grad school, a few days before New Year's Eve.

My black leather jacket did little to keep me warm with the wind chill, but it was a good luck charm—a "chick magnet," according to my friends, because women at the clubs liked to touch the soft, luxurious leather. I also wore a skintight short-sleeve black shirt that Zoey convinced me to buy, saying, "You spend so much time working out, you should show it off!" My hair was now short, spiky, and platinum blond, and rather than glasses I wore green colored contacts, to accentuate the green in my hazel eyes. I felt ready for the night with my Obsession for men cologne and black Doc Martens.

Lively voices enveloped us as we entered. As we moved toward the kitchen, women introduced themselves to us. About 25 lesbians surrounded us, all in their 20s, with a few gay guys sprinkled in. The upbeat music added to the lighthearted mood.

When we settled onto the couch, a woman with long blond hair sat next to me. I turned to her and said "Hi, I'm Kristin," and held out my hand.

"Hi, I'm Kate."

"Nice to meet you." I smiled at her and she smiled back.

She brushed her long hair behind her ears. Her silver top shimmered as she moved. "So, do you live around here?"

"I'm actually just in town for New Year's. I used to live in St. Louis when I went to Wash U for college, but I just moved to Houston about five months ago to go to grad school."

"What are you going to school for?"

"I just started a PhD program for Industrial and Organizational Psychology. I go to Rice University. What do you do?"

"I'm a high school teacher. I teach tenth grade English."

Her knee brushed up against mine and tingles spread across my skin. The decibel level in the apartment increased as more people arrived. We made small talk with a few people around us and grabbed another bottle of beer. Rainbow-colored holiday lights hung around the room, a Christmas tree lit up in the corner. I could smell the pine.

A group of women chatted behind us. My ears perked up when I heard an All-American-looking young woman say, "I'm a sophomore at Wash U right now and I'm in a sorority."

One of the other women asked her, "How is it being a lesbian in a sorority? That must be hard."

The sorority girl said, "Actually, I'm not out yet. I'm really worried that if I come out I could get ostracized or kicked out of my sorority." She stopped, shoulders slumped in her form-fitting sweater, and took another sip of beer. Looking down at the ground, she said, "I actually heard about a lesbian at Wash U who was in a sorority and brought her girlfriend to the sorority formal a few years ago."

I listened intently, my eyes widening.

She went on, "Apparently she even wrote an article for the student newspaper about being a lesbian."

I looked over at Zoey, who raised her eyebrows. I said nothing, but continued to listen.

The sorority girl said, "I heard that after she came out, they didn't kick her out of the sorority and she still had friends. It gives me hope that I might be able to come out. I'm not ready yet, but maybe at some point...."

I stood frozen, staring at the girl. When she started to walk away, I caught up to her and blurted out, "Hey, I heard what you said back there. I'm pretty sure I'm the sorority lesbian you were talking about." I paused and she stared at me. "I came out in my sorority and I wrote an article in the Wash U student newspaper about three years ago."

The sorority girl continued to stare at me, her eyes wide. "Really? That was you?"

"Yeah, that was me. I'm Kristin."

She broke into a huge smile, and put out her hand. "I'm Cheryl. So what was it like, coming out? What happened?"

"Well, it was really hard. Most of my sisters seemed ok with it, but some of my friendships just dried up. The biggest thing that helped me was going to GLBA, the gay group on campus."

After talking with Cheryl for a while, Zoey was ready to leave for another party. "It was great to meet you," I told Cheryl. "Good luck and hang in there. I promise you will get through it."

She smiled and waved goodbye.

Zoey and I arrived at the Jewish Community Center's Lesbian New Year's Eve party. We grabbed plastic flutes of champagne then entered the massive dance hall, where crowds of women danced to disco and pop. We all danced with abandon, groups of us dirty dancing with each other, hips gyrating and arms wrapped around each other.

We saw Kate and a few others from the party and joined them on the dance floor. When a slow song came on, Kate looked at me and said, "Do you want to dance?"

"Sure!"

She placed her arms around my neck and smiled at me. I wrapped my arms around her waist, pulling her close. I could smell her floral-scented perfume.

Other women began coupling up as well, until the floor was packed with lesbians slow dancing. We moved in closer and I could feel Kate's warm body pressed against mine. I looked around. All the couples were locked in embrace, focused only on each other as we swayed to the music.

I thought back to my first slow dance with Sarah at the pajama party junior year. Even now I could remember vividly how uncomfortable I felt, surrounded by judgment and stares.

I shook off the unpleasant memories and brought my focus back to the present. I felt the softness of Kate's cheek against mine, closed my eyes, and sank into the song, letting my body relax into the music and into her body. Here, at this moment, I knew I truly belonged.

ACKNOWLEDGMENTS

First of all, I want to thank the writing teachers and fellow students who saw the potential in me and encouraged me to write. My first narrative non-fiction course at UCLA taught by Alison Singh Gee helped me find the genre (memoir) I knew I was meant to write. My teacher at a memoir writing course at UC Berkeley, Margo Perin, told me, "A friend of mine has a daughter in junior high school who was struggling with her identity as a lesbian. She just committed suicide. Please keep writing because people need to hear your story." This always stuck with me and got me through the multiple rounds of edits.

I'd also like to thank my editor, Teja Watson, and my cover designer, Vanessa Mendozzi, as well as others in the writing community that provided advice along the way—Mark Matousek and Lisa Cornelio.

A special thanks to everyone I wrote about in the book, who provided friendship, love, support, and understanding during a time when I struggled with my sexuality and gender identity. In particular, I would like to thank my college roommate, all my GLBA friends, many women from my sorority pledge class, and my two boyfriends in college. All of you helped me through an emotional roller-coaster. And thanks to my first and second girlfriends, two intense loves I still remember fondly. From the bottom of my heart, I want you to know I am truly sorry for not being the best girlfriend I could have been. And thank you to my parents and sister, who have been so supportive of me throughout the years.

Finally, I want to thank friends and family that gave me feedback on my book, including my parents, sister, Nancy Q., Wiley, Sarah V., Angela S., and Shannon B. And last but not least, my wife, Sandy Yen, who endured many weekends, evenings, and very early mornings for almost 10 years when I spent time writing instead of being with her. I couldn't have done it without her support!

AUTHOR BIO

Kristin Griffith has authored several publications on LGBTQ topics, founded the LGBT graduate student, faculty, and staff organization at Rice University, and facilitated support groups at the Los Angeles LGBT Center. Kristin holds an MBA in Marketing from UCLA and has worked in tech companies including Netflix, Intuit, and Adobe. She lives in Oakland with her wife and two rescue dogs.

www.kristingriffith.com

Made in the USA
Las Vegas, NV
11 March 2022

45440527R00177